OCEAN
CROSSING
WAYFARER

Second Edition

OCEAN
CROSSING
WAYFARER

**TO ICELAND AND NORWAY
IN A 16FT OPEN BOAT**

Second edition

FRANK AND MARGARET DYE

ADLARD COLES NAUTICAL · LONDON

'It is the bliss of ignorance that tempts the fool, but it is he who sees the wonders of the earth.'

'It is in the nature of all of us, or is it just my own peculiar makeup which brings, when the wind blows, that queer feeling, mingled longing and dread? A thousand invisible fingers seem to be pulling me, trying to draw me away from the four walls where I have every comfort, into the open where I shall have to use my wits and my strength to fool the sea in its treacherous moods, to take advantage of fair winds and to fight when I am fairly caught – for a man is a fool to think he can conquer nature.'

Frederic 'Frite' Fenger cruised his 17ft sailing canoe in the Caribbean, Grenada and the Virgin Islands singlehanded in 1917. The boat is in a museum at Bruce Mines, Ontario, Canada.

Published by Adlard Coles Nautical
an imprint of A & C Black Publishers Ltd
38 Soho Square, London W1D 3HB
www.adlardcoles.com

First published by David & Charles (Publishers) Ltd 1977
Reprinted 1978, 1979
Second edition published by Adlard Coles Nautical 2006
Reprinted 2008

ISBN 13: 978-0-7136-7568-9

A CIP catalogue record for this book is available from the British Library.

A & C Black uses paper produced with elemental chlorine-free pulp, harvested from managed sustainable forests.

Typeset in Palatino
Printed and bound by WKT

Frontispiece: *Wanderer* leaving the uninhabited island of Pabbay, Outer Hebrides for a night passage to St Kilda.

Contents

Dedication

For *Wanderer* and the National Maritime Museum, Falmouth.

Wanderer *in her final home, the National Maritime Museum, Falmouth* (Chris Sayers).

Foreword to the First Edition

The sailing exploits of Frank Dye and his wife Margaret are already known to thousands in many parts of the world. Yet to understand fully these cruises, why they are made and how they bring joy and satisfaction to these very skilled dinghy sailors, you really need to meet and know them. This book goes some of the way towards giving this insight into the compelling motivation that overcomes the hardship, discomfort and even fear which is the virtually inevitable accompaniment of such major cruises in notoriously difficult waters.

My feeling is that this book only goes some of the way towards giving the insight I mention. It is unavoidable that this is so if the accounts are to be written by the Dyes themselves – as they most certainly should be. They are by nature incredibly modest, emphasising mistakes rather than achievements, embroidering nothing, starkly matter of fact. This should be ever-present at the back of your mind as you read this book.

Above all, please do not think that Frank Dye is a reckless fanatic who chooses to sail in perilous places just to see if he can and to prove his ability to survive some fairly advanced form of self-inflicted torture. He prepares his cruises with meticulous care and, perhaps having chosen a potentially dangerous area in which to sail for reasons which will be explained later, he does his utmost to reduce the dangers by good sound seamanship, which includes the foresight and caution that goes with experience.

Why does he choose to go to these geographically inhospitable places? It is because small boats have always been a part of such places since before the Vikings. It is also because, if you arrived by ship or aeroplane as a visitor in such places, you would remain as a stranger watched from behind closed doors, but if you land from a 16ft (4.88m) dinghy, you are immediately taken into the houses and hearts of the people and get to know them as you could probably never do otherwise. This is perhaps the only way in which someone from the well-insulated modern world can get a glimpse at and the feel of that remarkable period of seafaring in which the Viking made such an impression.

It is a little sad that these following pages tell only of *Wanderer's* ocean crossings, for she has been the Dyes' partner in so much other sailing that may not be quite as impressive, but is full of interest, originality and achievement – quite often flavoured with peace and quietude instead of rugged struggles with wind and sea. To me, that is all *Wanderer* and Frank and Margaret, and no part is more absorbing than the rest. Let us hope they will write about it all sometime.

A few years ago *Wanderer* sailed up to the bottom of my garden on the Hamble River, off the Solent. I had no idea they were coming, although I did know that they were sailing westwards along the English south coast from East Anglia. I happened to be in the garden that evening and I don't know why, but although there were then about 4,000 Wayfarer dinghies like *Wanderer* in existence and although the Hamble is full of sailing boats on the move almost all the time, I instantly recognised her when she was still about a quarter mile away, creeping over the shallows against the swiftly ebbing stream.

'We've come to take you for a sail,' they said. 'Not just now, you won't,' I replied, as the water uncovered the mud flats and left *Wanderer* high and dry. 'Next sailing 4am tomorrow morning.' So we fed and talked and laughed that evening and were up before the sun as the water flooded over the marsh to lift *Wanderer* up again. I shall never forget the peace of that early morning on the Solent as we sailed along, brewing tea as *Wanderer* skipped happily over the scarcely ruffled water. This was another side to the character of the Dyes' cruises that is less known and slips by unnoticed, yet is more within the ability of many to emulate and enjoy themselves.

Designing boats is my happiest occupation. And as each is designed, I seem to conjure up a vision of the chaps working to build the boat, the kind of people who will sail her, the conditions and the places in which she will sail and how she will cope with them – for these are the people and the situations which will make the design come to life. I must confess that as I drew out the Wayfarer design I never visualised her riding out a gale on the way to Iceland, nor did I ever think that two such remarkable people as Frank and Margaret Dye would sail in her. They certainly have breathed an abundance of life into the Wayfarer design – and in return *Wanderer* has become a part of their lives.

Ian Proctor
February 1977

Preface to the Second Edition

Forty years ago I began sailing *Wanderer*, our Wayfarer sailing dinghy, on coastal and river cruises. In fact we were out every week-end learning, summer and winter, irrespective of weather fair and foul, and as our experience increased this developed into offshore passages. It was a slow gaining of knowledge which continues today.

Some four decades later I wonder what has changed? What has altered? What did I learn and when? With the benefit of hindsight what would I have changed? What mistakes? What pleasures? And was it worth it? What would I now do differently?

Since I was a small boy I have read endlessly about small boat voyages, about tough men, seamen and fishermen. No-one in the family sailed. We lived 40 miles from the sea, and my only experience of boats as a child was when my elderly grandfather took me out in his river punt when he wasn't 'babbing for eels of an evenin'; paddling a child's canoe in the waves on the beach at Bacton; watching the fishermen launching off the beach; and, pleasure of pleasures – being asked if I'd like to go out with them for the day line fishing. I stood on the shore and dreamed of what lay beyond the next headland, and what lay invisible over the horizon.

Building up the family business which had run down during the war allowed me no time to follow my interest. Thus I was 27 years old before I again set foot in a boat and it almost ended in disaster. On impulse I bought an aluminium alloy 12ft (3.65m) sailing dinghy, lugsail rigged, with cotton sails and galvanised steel centreboard for £40. This sum was not a lot of money even in those days, and to me she looked 'a good boat and useful'. My father offered to crew, and Sunday saw us lauching onto Wroxham Broad with little idea of what we were doing. 'Get that damn'd tin boat off my starting-line. NOW!' roared the Tannoy from the prestigious Yacht Club amongst the sound of booming cannon, for all to hear.

Mortified, on Monday I put the 'damned tin boat' up for sale. Obviously a tin boat was not acceptable amongst the sailing community, and I almost gave up sailing. Selling it was a mistake, for with hindsight, I now realise it was fitted for cruising and would have served me well.

So what has changed? The sea, the sailors, the boats, the equipment, the weather? Certainly the sea has not changed at all. It is still just as uncaring, uncontrollable and dangerous as it ever was, and the penalty for 'getting it wrong' is very high.

The men and women *have* changed, and now the emphasis is more on competition. Racing takes place at every sailing club every weekend, and there is vast investment in offshore competition by way of sponsorship. Fortunately many still sail for pure pleasure, and others like *Wanderer* set out to learn the ways of wind and weather and to explore other parts and understand the coastal communities.

Frank learning the techniques of crossing a bar at Brancaster Staithe in North Norfolk in Wanderer (Eastern Daily Press).

Acknowledgements

Although I am responsible for the text of the first edition of this book and for the new chapters in this edition, it is a genuine joint effort because I used Frank's log books. Frank on his longer cruises has always kept a comprehensive log written up at the end of each watch and full of the kind of detail that no-one has time to record at sea, especially in a Wayfarer in heavy weather. Although I did not accompany him on the passages to Iceland and Norway, we have sailed many hundreds of miles together in *Wanderer* and it was relatively easy, with his assistance, to catch the flavour of these two trips – as I hope I have done.

We are most grateful to Ian Proctor for permission to reproduce the plans of his Wayfarer design and his appendix on the design of the Wayfarer.

All photographs and illustrations are our own except when stated to the contrary.

Margaret Dye

PART I

WANDERER'S CREWS
AND EXPERIENCE GAINED

Wanderer's *Crews and*
Experience Gained

Offshore cruising in an open boat can be hard, cold, wet, lonely, and occasionally miserable, but it is exhilarating too. To take an open dinghy across a hundred miles of sea, taking the weather as it comes; to know that you have only yourself and your mate to rely on in an emergency; to see the beauty of dawn creep across the ever restless and dangerous ocean; to make a safe landfall – is wonderful and all of these things develop a self-reliance that is missing from the modern, mechanical, safety-cautious civilised world.

I owe a great deal to my many crew – tough, adventurous and plain nice people. Invariably I have learned a great deal from them.

Bob Wright, a friend from school days, sailed with me on my first cruise from Brancaster Staithe to King's Lynn. With a fair wind and almost no knowledge of the ebb and flow of salt waters we were unable to stem the tide into Lynn Cut before dark. We dragged our Hornet, a 15ft (4.57m) racing machine, to the top of the sands and laid out an anchor so as to swing clear of the shipping channel during the night. I remember being badly scared in the early hours watching navigation lights heading straight for us and swinging away at the last moment to follow the channel (and we were without any means of showing our presence).

Surprisingly Bob crewed for me again at Easter to the Humber. This was an ambitious project as we had not learned to reef afloat and were equipped with wet weather gear of gas capes, cycle leggings, and gym shoes.

We departed Brancaster Staithe on the last of the ebb tide, crossed the Wash with a small reef in the mainsail and pulled the Hornet ashore onto the sea wall at Chapel St Leonard in Lincolnshire some

5 hours later, and rigged the tent alongside the dinghy. Next day we headed north with the weather unsettled, the wind freshening and the dinghy beginning to plane. We planned to cross the mouth of the Humber and pull ashore for the night in Yorkshire.

Extract from the Log

Bob overboard! We had been planing in rushes for some time with Bob on the end of the sliding seat. A sudden gust, the Hornet heeled, Bob's gym shoes slipped off the wet gunwhale, he slid down the plank into the water – and was gone! I just managed to keep the dinghy upright although she was much over-canvased. Scared of capsizing due to my lack of weight, I was afraid of losing sight of my crew in the choppy sea. I came alongside him at the second attempt but his clothing was so sodden with water that he was too heavy to climb over the transom and the Hornet was too tender to bring him aboard over the side. After several attempts I tied him to the stern and sailed him ashore to get him back in the boat – a distance of something over a mile.

By the time we were off Donna Nook, the southern entrance of the Humber, the wind was heavy and we rolled in a deep reef and tied down the jib. (We had to come ashore to do this as we had not yet learned to reef afloat.) We estimated the wind to be almost gale force, as we were showing only 30% of our sail area, and would dearly have liked to pull ashore until it blew out, but it was only just after low water, the gently shelving beach floods for over a mile, and with no shelter from the wind Bob was cold and shivering violently after his swim.

I had read that a boat should stay in deep water to make maximum use of the flood tide, so we stood out into the deep water channel. It was a mistake. The tide was running into the eye of the wind and we were soon in heavy breaking seas. Badly scared, we stood back close under the shore – and so we learned the importance of getting a lee from the land!

Members of that most hospitable sailing club the Grimsby & Cleethorpes Sailing Club met us at the water's edge and helped us ashore. We were shivering with cold and Bob was unable to walk. They carried him into the clubhouse, lit a fire, found us dry clothes, filled us with hot food and whiskey, then returned across the sands to carry our boat up to the clubhouse. We were too cold to do it ourselves. Later they banked up the fire, gave us the keys and told us to sleep in the warm.

Next morning the forecast was 'Winds gusting up to 20 knots from the SW, veering gradually to NW and becoming light by evening'. Several club members had given us dire warnings of the violence of the race off Spurn Point known as The Binks, and they recommended we arrive at slack water. We slept late, and after planing across the Humber, turned Spurn Point two hours late. With no warning at all we were in heavy breaking seas – great lumps of water rising suddenly all round us and collapsing in every direction. We luffed each breaker and when we worked clear were amazed to find we had shipped only about fifteen gallons, but were badly frightened.

At Hornsea in Yorkshire we went ashore to find coffee and hot food, leaving the Hornet anchored in three feet. On our return she was full of water, sand and children. The holidaymakers told us she had rolled over on her own in the slight swell, and the children were bailing out and putting our gear back into the boat. We were thankful that it hadn't happened when we were sleeping at anchor. It was still typically cold Easter weather so we called it a day.

Hitch-hiking home, Bob and I compared our impressions of the trip. We had proved that it was possible to cruise in a dinghy with reasonable safety, sailed in winds of 35 knots – and this in the Humber where conditions are notorious – met our first tidal race, and concluded that races are best avoided. I was horrified how easily a person can go overboard and that a man is invisible at 80 yards in a seaway. Lifelines or lifejackets would be worn in heavy weather in future. Our gas capes and cycle leggings were woefully inadequate; there is no alternative to proper seagoing oilskins.

I have always had a healthy respect for the sea and a dislike of water, and now I was beginning to learn that it could be dangerous as well as frightening. Yet we'd also had a great deal of fun!

We had made mistakes; but already the sea fascinated me and I thought deeply about what I wanted to do. I had reservations about the Hornet as a cruising boat. With the benefit of experience I cannot now think of a more unsuitable dinghy in which to cruise, for she was extremely wet, almost impossible to sleep in, unstable at anchor, tender, and when we shipped water it ran forward so she was likely to run her bows under in a seaway.

In the autumn I retired to the safety of the Norfolk Broads, racing with Norwich Frostbites for the winter. I had found the sea to be a very lonely and frightening place.

The following January, fascinated by the ability of my new Wayfarer, I planned to sail instead of trailing from Barton Broad to Norwich to race with Norwich Frostbites for the rest of the winter season.

Bob crewed and we sailed in freezing conditions down to Great Yarmouth and next day carried our tide through Breydon to leave the dinghy at Mr Odie's boatyard at Brundall. We had a 300yd (274m) struggle along the lane through 12-inch (30.4-cm) deep flood water, ice covered and too thick to break a way through but not quite thick enough to bear our weight at each step. We were wearing canvas sailing shoes, we couldn't hurry as we had been told there were deep dykes each side of the lane, it was half a mile to the rail station and I could no longer feel my legs. Fortunately the station porter allowed us to dry out in front of his fire, and after a meal in Norwich we returned home. My log book tells me that Mr Odie broke the ice round *Wanderer* daily for two weeks and replaced our cotton mooring lines which broke from ice and chafe with terylene ones for a charge of only 15 shillings, whereas I noted that I would have been happy to pay 35 shillings or even £2! John Buckingham and I completed the sail to Norwich two weeks later when the ice cleared.

Keith Carter, like me, sailed at Denver Sluice. He had just taken up sailing and, at 19, was the youngest of my adventurous crews. He was a member of a local family firm so it was very convenient for planning.

I was beginning to realise how cold it was at sea and the need to sleep warm. We found two ex-RAF aircrew survival suits in the Government Surplus store – down-filled sleeping bags with separate arms and a rubberised outer cover with gloves attached and with a transparent visor to enable a ditched airman to work in warmth in his rubber dinghy. We tried them out on his parents' lawn one February night. I shall always remember the startled language of the milkman next dawn as he opened the gate and tripped over two frost covered mummified figures on the grass!

We planned carefully – a cruise from Brancaster Staithe after we finished work, crossing the Wash, and anchoring for the night off Skegness, then sailing up the east coast to Scotland. It would be sheltered sailing with a prevailing southwesterly wind off the land, through an area that was little known in those days. Cliffs, rocky reefs and deep water replacing the sands and shallows we were used to, but if I wanted to cruise further afield it was a type of sailing I had to master.

It was a cruise that went perfectly from start to finish.

All our gear worked superbly, and an enthusiastic efficient crew made sailing a pleasure, so extended cruising was 'on the cards' for the future. I was beginning to realise how important compatibility was in the close confines of a dinghy.

Shortly after I was embarrassed by a comment in *Yachting Monthly*: 'I hear that Frank Dye, a member of Norwich Frostbite S C, who sailed his 16ft Wayfarer from Brancaster to Dunbar, has planned another ambitious sea cruise. He is a little reticent about his plans but I gather a North Sea crossing is one of his ambitions. Knowing Mr Dye and the care he takes with the preparations and careful planning that goes into them, I would not in the least be surprised to hear that he has achieved his ambition.'

I had no wish for the pressure of publicity.

John Buckingham was vastly more experienced than me, a professional PE teacher, an experienced sailing instructor, and I was lucky to have him as my mentor – laconic, intelligent and fascinated by small boats and their behaviour at sea. Like me, he was prepared to accept discomfort and calculated risks in order to learn. We sailed and learned a little more each time.

We discussed the problems of cruising an open boat at sea and, planning carefully, decided on a trial cruise across the southern North Sea to Holland, then skirting the Friesian Islands to Denmark (see map page 20). In the event of a gale we would lower the mast into a crutch, put out the sea anchor to pull her through the breaking waves, and remove the rudder (the boat would be drifting astern). We also fitted a canvas cockpit cover in order to shed water and spray back where it belonged and to give us some protection from the elements. 'Then it is merely a case of relaxing and sleeping until the gale blows out, then carry on,' we reasoned.

This experiment turned out to be a brutal initiation into bad weather, and only the greater toughness and experience of my crew carried us through. My log says:

NW GALE IN GERMAN BIGHT. *Wanderer's* crew John Buckingham.

We cannot set course for Heligoland not knowing our exact position off Holland, for if we miss it and the weather deteriorates further we should be too near a dangerous lee shore, so we sail NE expecting to make a landfall at Sylt at teatime. Very relieved to hear (as we believed) that weather will not deteriorate – however if it does we shall have sea room!

07.30 Wind NNW force 6/7 and increasing, sea rising. Took several photos of John sailing, but am doubtful of readings exposure meter gives me.

08.30 Wind force 6/7 but we free off slightly to NE and both sitting out *Wanderer* smokes along throwing a ½ bucket of spray aboard as she meets each sea. Sea increasing but not yet dangerous. Change to one hour watches – constant attention to waves is tiring. Speed 6/7 knots and self baler working well. I find the hiss of breaking crests to windward and the roar of waves going away downwind unnerving.

10.30 Wind dies to steady force 6 and I make large cheese sandwich each. John says he must congratulate Ian Proctor on designing 'A marvellous sea boat'. About to have a tot of rum when wind pipes up to steady force 7. Seas building up and breaking heavily.

We have stuck our necks out and now we are going to catch it! I know real fear, but watch John sailing, calm and competent, and regain my confidence – what a wonderful crew he is!

No more driving to windward but a case of luffing seas as necessary and working NE. Wind backing slightly. Several crests break down on us but centreboard is half raised and dinghy slips sideways. Self baler a godsend and keeps boat dry. Patches of very bad sea – uneven bottom?

12.30 Extremely heavy seas – wind NNW and we are working N. Decide to free off to see effect of seas beam on. *Wanderer* jumps to 10/12 knots and impossible to hold when a breaker roars down on her. Waves 10/12ft with hollow tumbling faces and sea a mass of white. I would not have believed a dinghy could sail in such conditions. John – 'What a bloody wonderful boat, thank God!'

I do not think we dare approach the Danish coast in these conditions but will have to beat about off the coast until the seas die down.

13.00 Sudden increase force 8. The howling of the wind goes up another notch and boat unable to luff – just moves sideways. Several seas break down heavily on us but *Wanderer* rose to each magnificently but staggered up the last 4ft and I expect any wave to drive us astern and capsize us. John got out the drogue and threw over bows on end of 120ft nylon rope at same time lowering the mainsail while I removed the rudder and lifted the centreboard and self baler. Tore right hand on mainsheet block but didn't notice blood until later. While rigging crutch and lowering mast, the masthead touched water and burgee torn off (great pity to lose Norwich Frostbite burgee for I have done all my cruising under it). I was sick as I tied cover down to first eyelet and again at each one as I worked aft – so was John.

Wanderer riding well with slight snatch as drogue pulls her over each breaking crest and occasionally jumps sideways as a cross sea catches her. Waves 15/16ft. No idea of drift – hope max 1 kt.

15.00 Dutch trawler works across to ask if assistance required. Show Red Ensign and shout 'OK'. He says nearest land 25 miles – great relief. Wonderful seamanship – pitching and rolling insanely with bows rising 25ft and crashing down but keeps within 20ft of our masthead. Violently seasick.

Seas increasing. We hear each wave roar down on us, feel *Wanderer* rise and hear rattle of spray on the cover and then feel the bows drop. Are better if we lie on the floorboards unmoving and I am better face down. Violently seasick as soon as we move, and then sweat and shiver. Conditions much as I had imagined them.

John has torn oilskins and is soaked and fearing exposure. I crawl forward to get dry clothing from forward buoyancy. Take cup to be sick into but over jib and floorboards. John makes several attempts to change with consequent seasickness – gives it up.

Dusk. Seas 20ft and roaring down on us in great lines of white.

Tuesday 2nd August. I remember John asking for flare during darkness but too cold and tired to care. Trawler almost ran us down and passed within oar's length. Thank God he missed our drogue! Light on quarter during night but too seasick to check with chart apart from noting flashes. I remember being sick over stern while checking flashes and being fascinated by the lines of phosphorescence roaring away downwind – a beautiful and awe inspiring sight.

05.30 Daylight. Seas as bad but dinghy riding well. 130 strokes of pump clear her. Begin to worry about sea room and plan what to do.

Only solution to use our distress signals and hope to drive safely through the surf on drogue, releasing our two tins of oil: consider anchoring offshore but decide this will pull her bows down too much. John crawls forward to close the hatch but stores have shifted and jammed the cover and seasickness defeats him; also shortens drogue warp which has chafed. Manage to sleep occasionally – must be getting our sea legs.

11.00 I crawl forward for water and drag it aft – only 9ft but it seems miles! Stink forward where I was sick last night very bad and I hang over transom retching.

14.50 Wind dies to force 7 and decide to change into dry clothes, more sickness but eventually done. Sun comes out and wet clothing tied down in wind. Wind force 6 dying. Seas no longer breaking heavily.

16.00 Flotilla of German frigates pass 1½ miles to eastward and tail-end-Charlie returns to ask if we require assistance. Told in excellent English, 'Weser light eight miles south' and he backs away so as to avoid our drogue and joins the rest of the flotilla circling 2 miles north. We mark up our chart and realise Heligoland is 11 miles north close-hauled.

17.40 Sailing – sickness gone and replaced by hunger.

John's conclusions are interesting, particularly his reservation (which he underlined twice). 'We learned a great deal, and there is still much to record concerning living aboard a dinghy at sea, feeding in all weathers, navigation, keeping fit and our general conclusions about deep sea cruising in a dinghy, which certainly appears to be a practical proposition, *provided the crew are sufficiently experienced.*'

He sailed with me the following year too.

John sailed with me again, across the northern part of the North Sea from Rosehearty in Scotland to Bergen in Norway. It was a 300 mile crossing in almost continuous fresh to strong winds from dead astern – a very fast crossing, taking just under 3 days including 8 hours lying to a sea anchor. In spite of the overcast weather it was exhilarating sailing, with no effort required apart from an occasional reef, and navigation was easy – just ticking off the miles; but we discovered the dangers of running too fast in big seas when *Wanderer* gybed, broached and filled when I was off duty asleep under the head cover. At 2010 hours I woke up with the idea something was wrong and shouted a question to John at the tiller. 'I said bail like hell, we're bloody well full!' he shouted back.

Apparently *Wanderer* had gybed with a breaking crest under her stern, broached-to, half filled, straightened up, gybed heavily, broached again and filled completely. Being fast asleep and well wedged in I did not realise what had happened and when it dawned I broke the shock cord holding the head cover and 'bailed like hell'. My glasses had disappeared – probably washed under floorboards. *Wanderer* was no longer in danger, for with the weight of water aboard she was almost stopped, and the fore and aft buoyancy lockers were lifting her easily over each sea.

John forced the dinghy back on to course, now running at a more reasonable speed because of weight of water, and we set about bailing. Once the level was down to the floorboards, we put the self-bailer down to suck out the rest and then took in the reefed mainsail and ran off under the bare mast while I rigged the small jib. We were under way half an hour later – dry, stowed, and the only loss my glasses, but I had a spare pair fortunately. It was surprising neither of

We set about jury-rigging the dinghy, having cut off the base of the mast and shortened the standing rigging with the dinghy rolling heavily. Illustration by Winston Megoran by kind permission of *Yachting Monthly.*

us had got wet, but we had lashings round the wrists and ankles of our oilskins and also round our waists, although I was damp in the small of my back and under my armpits below the vent holes; we were lucky that John was not thrown into the sea.

Had we been reaching, *Wanderer* would have coped with the conditions easily, but discussing it over a hot supper we began to appreciate that when running before the wind it is easy to overpower the boat without realising it's happening.

Rod Thompson was an American serviceman who raced a Firefly dinghy successfully and often noisily at Denver Sailing Club at Denver sluice in the Fens and he sailed a Silhouette locally. He was a competent sailor and regularly beat me on handicap, but I hesitated to sail with him for a long time because of the differences of approach of Americans in so many things. To give Rod some experience sailing *Wanderer*, John Galloway and I organised a Sunday dinghy cruise across the Wash (John was another friend who had taught me so much when I started sailing and we often crewed for one another). Conditions were poor verging on rough, and there was enough sea running to make it risky to beach all the dinghies through the surf, so we anchored them offshore and I collected their crews on the theory that *Wanderer* was the best sea boat and we'd get everyone ashore 'in one go'. By the same reasoning I sailed in under the mainsail, whereas it would have been more sensible to run in under genoa. *Wanderer* surfed in, put her bow down into the preceding wave and 'ran under' with 9 men and a boy aboard. Capsizing, she ran her mast into the bottom. A cursory check of the boat and we stripped off, much to the amusement of the holidaymakers, dried our clothes, ate fish and chips under the pier and returned.

Departing Rosehearty a week later, close-hauled, with Rod as crew, bound for Norway, *Wanderer* was just able to weather the knife edged rocks at the harbour entrance without coming about. The following day 70 miles out, the wind headed us so we tacked, and the mast fell down! *Wanderer* looked a dreadful shambles with sail, rigging and spars trailing overside and rolling heavily in the swell – and all caused by a faulty rigging screw. I was so speechless I couldn't even swear, Rod grinning at my 'it can't happen to me' expression. The superficial check after the capsize on Skegness beach could have cost us our lives had we been forced to tack to clear the rocks leaving Rosehearty. The wood mast had broken at deck level, and I was glad of Rod's skill as a woodworker, not helped when I became seasick in the middle of the operation.

Approaching Utsire Island in a rising gale I decided to beat offshore to gain sea room as I was not certain that we could enter harbour safely with daylight fading and a heavy swell building. Rod didn't agree and argued until the boom gave him a resounding blow on the side of the head.

After several excellent days cruising through the fjords to Bergen and endless amusement watching Rod chatting up the Norwegian ladies ashore, we returned from Norway to London on a small Bergen Line general cargo ship with 8 passengers and *Wanderer* as deck cargo. The Captain agreed to lower us overboard at the nearest distance off Norfolk. We were up before dawn to find that he had altered course during the night and the ship was within sight of Corton light vessel. We used the jib and main sheets (doubled) as slings and climbed into the dinghy as the helmsman cut the engines and swung the ship in a half circle to give us a lee, while the first mate hoisted us on the ship's derrick. Even now I can remember the sinking feeling as we dropped down the steel side of the ship, slipped the hook, and pushed off before the swells carried us back onto the vertical steel wall now towering above us. We swung up the mast and hoisted sail as the sun rose. The crew and passengers had got up early to see us off and with shouts of 'likke til' from the deck and the bridge, we sailed for an England invisible beyond the horizon.

It goes without saying that it is essential not to upset the Customs and Immigration officers – they do not like being taken for granted and they do have a great deal of power. In those days, a sailing dinghy being dropped off from a freighter beyond the horizon was unusual – but we have always found them understanding, and helpful.

It had been an educational cruise and I thought carefully about it.

My carelessness in checking the boat after the capsize and missing the bent rigging screw could have been very serious and made me add safety lashing for the future. I had also given insufficient thought to food, as Americans have differing tastes; Rod disliked my preference for 'sharp' fruit such as tinned raspberries, currants and rhubarb, much preferring peaches and strawberries, and he hated eggs however cooked, which have always been the staple diet on *Wanderer*. Plus his brusque 'get up and go' occasionally grated. In his turn he disliked the English 'unnecessary caution' and 'excessive politeness'. We had some excellent sailing in the sheltered fjords, and ashore I found his 'hail fellow well met' attitude, especially chatting up the Norwegian ladies in true WWII GI fashion, a constant source of entertainment. It had been a successful cruise.

Bill Jacobs had a lifelong passion for the sea, was a man of enthusiasm, widely read, an efficient hospital manager and a most untypical Lay Preacher.

We planned a winter weekend sail along the North Norfolk coast to Cromer. My log reads:

The Sunday morning shipping forecast at 06.30 hrs was 'West to southwest Force 7–9'. I telephoned Bill Jacobs, but being cautious like me he had already phoned the Meteorological Office. Their version was 28–35 knots, a little south of west. Bill's comment was, 'not a gentlemanly type of sailing, but we aren't gentlemen – so let's go'.

With the wind in this direction there would be a slight lee from the land all the way along the Norfolk coast, and it was only this that made a passage possible in these gale conditions. However, we still planned carefully, for it is always foolish to take risks at sea, where the unexpected happens so quickly. The first decision was where to start?

Discarding other harbours for safety reasons we decided on Morston and launched into the narrow, muddy, lonely little creek winding through marshes towards Blakeney Pit and the grey tumult of the North Sea. In the deeper water of The Pit the larger boats were snubbing restlessly at their moorings. Closehauled now, there were sheets of spray being thrown up and blown back into the boat as our bows met each sea, and the wind shrilled in the shrouds. We were overcanvassed, even with the mainsail deep-reefed, but we needed the sail area to drive her through the short, breaking seas. This is always the problem of sailing to windward in heavy weather – too little sail and the boat is stopped by the seas – more sail and she is overpowered and risks a capsize.

Without the jib to help her round, *Wanderer* refused to tack, but Bill was overcoming this by reversing the rudder as she gathered sternway, so her head fell off on the new tack each time with certainty. This again is always a tricky manoeuvre in heavy weather, with the risk of capsize if a squall catches the boat before she regains steerage way. Bill is experienced though and made no mistakes, for which I was grateful, as the water looked very cold indeed.

Slowly we gained ground to windward to clear the tip of Blakeney Point and re-checked our preparations before facing the bar and the open sea. The small jib was ready for setting and would pull us ashore if we lost the mainsail because of a torn sail, broken blocks, or parted halyard; the CQR anchor was laid out on the floorboards ready for immediate use in case the mast went, for we had no wish to be blown out to sea to face the unpleasantness of a winter gale in the North Sea; the mainsail had been reefed from starboard and any further sail reduction would be done on the starboard tack, thus keeping the boat close under the shelter of the land. In the event of a capsize our lifejackets would keep us afloat until we could right the boat, and our lifelines would prevent us drifting away. We had timed our arrival at the bar for slack water, to avoid the unpleasant seas which would have built up earlier with the tide flooding against the wind.

At last we cleared the end of the Point and freed off for the run down the Harbour (the 'Harbour' is the deep water channel between the sandbanks). This was spectacular sailing, between two lines of broken water. To windward there was the seething line of white water where the seas were breaking heavily on the sandbanks protecting the Harbour from the west and, only 20 yards away to starboard, the waves were roaring on the beach. Between the two we were safe if nothing carried away.

Only one sea on the bar gave us any anxiety, but we were able to luff in good time before it broke. We then freed off round the wreck buoy into one of the most exciting downhill runs I can remember.

Looking back, the shallows of Blakeney Bar were a confused mass of breaking white water, throwing spray into the air and partially hiding the outline of the dark Norfolk hills behind a curtain of wind-blown spume. The tower of Blakeney church topped the low, lonely sandhills, the outline of the wide beaches was blurred by the wind driven sand, and everywhere there was the sound of the wind whistling out of the grey sky to drive us on our way. I remember the

Bill Jacobs takes his pleasures very seriously.

sight with pleasure – the restless dangerous sea, the lonely coast, the slate grey sky and the ever-present wind.

Further down the coast the dunes changed to the steep pebble beach at Salthouse, and we came onto the wind in order to turn down another reef, for the wind was still increasing. We eased the halliard and Bill tried to remove the next batten from the sail while I sat out to counteract his weight down to leeward. *Wanderer* was stopped, drifting sideways, heeling heavily, and shipping a lot of water in the gusts, and this rapidly became a test of endurance. It seemed to take hours to reef but was probably no more than ten minutes. Each time we seemed to be succeeding the wind tore the flogging sail out of our cold, numbed hands, and always the wind hammered us as we struggled. At last it was done; we turned down another three rolls in the mainsail and raced away for Cromer.

All too soon the mound of Beeston Hill was abeam and here a swell began to run into the coast from the north-west, obviously generated by gales further north, and the gap in the offshore banks between Blakeney Overfalls and Sheringham Shoals was allowing them to run unimpeded onto the beach. In the deeper water these were eight feet high, steep although not dangerous, but increasing in height as they reached the shallows – they could make beaching at Cromer too dangerous for a small boat and we might have to run further down the coast until we got a lee as the land tended more southerly.

Cromer is different from any other East Anglian town, and as it was my turn on the tiller I sailed past to enjoy the view. My inattention half filled the boat as an approaching squall caused an involuntary tack, the jib being taken aback. We beached safely in a smaller run of sea to pull *Wanderer* up the slipway to lie alongside the crab boats. I enjoyed the evening service and listened with pleasure to my crew, Bill, reading the lesson whilst outside the wild rough night buffeted the ancient church and emphasised the peace within. It was a memorable ending to a most enjoyable day.

We were gaining experience. I think it was Bill who quoted 'the sea has no favourites' and remarked '. . . and if you get into trouble you must be prepared to get yourself out of it by your own efforts'. It is a basic principle in cruising.

When I wrote up this trip to show the flexibility of a dinghy, the wide range of cruising ground available, and the pleasures that can be enjoyed even in winter in extreme conditions I thought I had emphasised the careful preparation that is essential. Perhaps not, as it attracted some harsh criticism in the correspondence columns.

Margaret has an impish sense of humour and an intense interest in the sea and smaller boats (having suffered from large yachts and big crews). She is quick witted with a spontaneous enthusiasm and an appreciation of beauty, music and art and a liking for the warmer climes. She was soon made Wayfarer cruising secretary, and using her teaching experience she introduced Wayfarer Winter Training Weekends (first held at Cowes and then at my marina until they outgrew it), Wayfarer Rallies and a library of logs that had won cruising trophies.

Always ready to take on an adventure, she must have been alarmed to be deposited with *Wanderer* at the ferry terminal at Newcastle upon Tyne, with instructions to trans-ship at Bergen and telephone me when she arrived at the Lofoten Islands in Northern Norway!

Her story of the London Dock strike gives the story from her point of view:

Arctic Norway Cruise

One year when there was a dock strike *Wanderer* was locked in the London docks for the whole of July, so our plan to ship her to Bergen, sailing on towards the Polar Circle, was impossible. Much too late in the sailing season when the strike broke, Frank collected *Wanderer* from London docks and drove north to the North Sea ferry port at Newcastle upon Tyne. I was shipped with the dinghy and trailer and told only to get *Wanderer* from Bergen to the Lofoten Islands, and then telephone Frank's Norfolk business, so that he could join me. He arrived by seaplane just as I was watching our Wayfarer being craned into the water.

A day later we sailed out of a calm, windless Svolvaer harbour. A helicopter seaplane and sea eagle left at the same time, and barely cleared our mast.

We spent the first day dozing and rowing and wondering about katabatic winds, whirlpools and fjords a half-mile deep and 3000ft high. The blue Arctic landscape was impressive, and seemed to stretch into infinity the air was so clear; one mountain range rising into the next with glaciers white tinged with turquoise falling off their peaks. The silence was frighteningly and wonderfully impressive. At 03.00 hrs next day the sun had not set, and the icing sugar-like glaciers were just tipped with orange. It was too hot to sleep; we had already stripped off our Arctic clothing, replacing the Damart layers with cotton coverings – so we set sail. There was not a breath of wind. We recalled all the warnings we had received about not dinghy cruising in the Arctic – where all the locals used motor boats, as there was either no wind or too much.

Then, quite suddenly, we both became ensnared by the magic of the Arctic. Its isolation, vastness and silence is something to be experienced, not explained. We rowed on for ten hours, and anchored off Tjeldsund. Putting up the tent beneath a large ice field in brilliant sunshine, we fell asleep, awaking later as a full faced moon, yellow, open and unblinking, filled the tent with tranquil moonshine.

Three weeks later after wonderful light wind, warm air, 24 hour daylight sailing through the 'Arctic Alps', and meeting friendly people, the sudden late August storms brought snow; our holiday time was up. Had our original plans to ship *Wanderer* to Bergen then sail on towards Trondheim happened, we should never have reached the Arctic. The dock strike delayed our schedule, and so by adapting plans, and shipping *Wanderer* further north, we had actually had a far more excitingly remote cruise.

Margaret enjoying the peace of the Arctic.

PART II

ICELAND

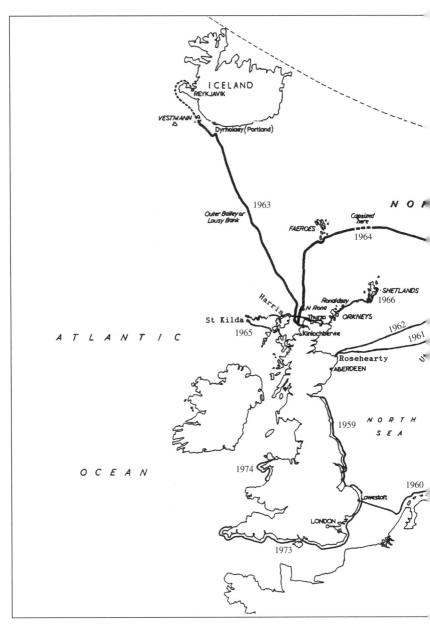

Track charts to Iceland and Norway. Previously Wanderer had sailed along most of the coasts bordering the North Sea and crossed direct from Scotland to Norway, but

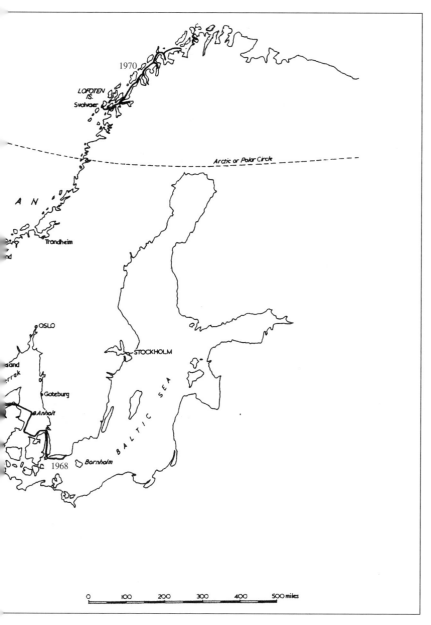

1970

LOFOTEN
IS.
Svolvaer

Arctic or Polar Circle

A N

Trondheim
nd

OSLO
sånd
rrak
Goteburg
Anholt
1968   Bornholm

STOCKHOLM

BALTIC SEA

0   100   200   300   400   500 miles

the 1963 and 1964 passages were something rougher and tougher.

1

Vikings' Trail

'It is only 650 miles (1,046km) to Iceland: it's a dangerous landfall, but it might be an interesting cruise.' John Buckingham and I had just sailed *Wanderer* across the North Sea from Scotland to Bergen and then northwards through the fjords to Aalesund; but instead of the usual pleasant fjord sailing, the weather had been atrocious – undoubtedly the worst weather we had experienced on any cruise to date. However, we had gained a great deal of experience, and I was beginning already to think of next year's cruise.

'The open-water passage from north-west Scotland to Iceland presents few problems and ought to take approximately ten days, so we would provision for eighteen; we could expect two gales . . .' I continued my musing, but unfortunately John, my excellent sailing companion, had other commitments for the following year. John had sailed with me on the last two cruises across the North Sea and I thought him the ideal crew. He taught physical education at the local secondary school, in the town where I was general manager of my father's Ford Main Dealership. Being over 6ft (1.83m) tall and very strong, he had obvious assets, but also he was intelligent, humorous, an excellent worker, easy to get on with, and an expert seaman, again like me self-taught, both of us having gained most of our sea experience off the north Norfolk coast.

Choice of crew is more important than weather, cruising ground, boat, or any other consideration. There was one occasion between Stadt and Aalesund towards the end of our sail to Norway when I was utterly exhausted and therefore very irritable. John must have felt equally bad, but instead of arguing he gave me a couple of hours sleeping off watch. A damned fine crew, I doubt there can be a better!

Throughout the winter I continued to plan. In fact, even before the end of the cruise in Norwegian waters, I was planning next year's trip. In spite of the shocking weather conditions on that trip I should go north again. I realised that with my annual holiday restricted to two weeks it was impossible to reach the Arctic Circle by sailing through the Norwegian fjords, so instead I thought of the following possible trips:

1 From east Scotland to north Norway, possibly calling at the Shetlands. A long hard trip. The Norwegian sea could be unpleasant but it would bring the Arctic Circle within our reach. This was a cruise that appealed to me enormously but beyond my competence at that time.
2 From east Scotland to Fair Isle and across to the Faeroes. Very interesting cruise, but I disliked those short open-water passages, for we should rarely be a sufficiently safe distance from land to ride out an unexpected on-shore gale nor close enough to land before beaching became impossible due to the surf.
3 From west Scotland (Outer Hebrides) to St Kilda and across to southern Iceland. This appealed to me greatly – but it was a rough hard cold area and meant a 600-mile (804.65-km) open-sea passage.

I had considered buying a sextant and learning to use it; in fact I had already been offered a good sextant by the Admiralty Chart Agents E Brown (Depot) of London for £45 but still hesitated as it was a big outlay for only two weeks' use. Most of the radio beacons are on the western side of Iceland (including several aircraft beacons) and one is situated on the southern coast. Thus it should be possible to find Iceland safely by radio direction finding.

A study of the charts of the South Icelandic coast and reference to the *Pilot* confirmed that this was probably the most dangerous coast in Europe for a small open boat to make a landfall. The prevailing south-westerly winds turned the whole coast into a dangerous lee shore; the many glacial rivers flowed into coastal marshes where there was no vegetation; and the shelving sea bottom caused heavy seas and dangerous surf, rendering a landing risky, except in ideal conditions.

On the whole coast there was only one safe harbour, on the Vest-mann Islands, but since these islands were only 13 miles (20.92km) offshore they gave little sea-room in an emergency. The safest course was not to close the Icelandic coast, until there was a favourable weather forecast, preferably sailing along the south coast some 50 miles offshore and then slipping in behind Reykjanes and landing at Reykjavik. Closing the coast is always the most dangerous part of a cruise.

Normally I begin to suffer from 'cold feet' three to four weeks before a cruise, but this time I found that four months ahead of departure I was already feeling nervous. I had visions of sitting in the dinghy some 50 miles offshore with continuous south-westerly gales preventing a landing, then having to run for shelter in the lee of the Faeroes, tired, seasick and short of food.

I called at the Icelandic Tourist Office at 61 Piccadilly, London, and found them most helpful. There is a small population on the east coast centred around the fishing villages, and it would be possible to ship a boat back to England from there if necessary.

The North Atlantic has a well-earned reputation for bad weather. If the weather proved to be unsettled, such an extended cruise could prove an endurance test, and choice of crew was of supreme importance. By Easter I had an offer of a crew, and in May we spent a long weekend sailing together on an abortive cruise from Lowestoft to The Hague. We found ourselves unsuited and badly matched in temperament. The weather was appalling, I thought my crew was not sufficiently resistant to cold and, since he had a vast experience of dinghy cruising, we tended to argue. He probably thought me impossible anyway! The weather was cold, wet and rough with continual head winds. We beat halfway across, then admitted defeat and had a wild run back into the Thames estuary to Brightlingsea.

I discovered afterwards that two friends were out in the North Sea that same weekend. John Buckingham in a 5 tonner who also put back; and Peter Root who sailed back from Holland to Lowestoft in a 17ft (5.18m) Yachting World Rambler. He sailed 90 miles (144.83km) singlehanded in wild conditions on a dead run down to a particularly nasty low-lying lee shore and made a perfect landfall. It was a very fine piece of seamanship and when I saw him in Lowestoft harbour that evening he said it was 'a little unpleasant'!

Other prospective crews I shied away from, as they tended to think they knew it all, and looked down their noses at the ultra-cautious dinghy cruising types. Crew trouble! It is the nightmare of all cruising skippers. I continually rang round my friends, but they all had other holiday plans. Eventually, with only weeks to go before my sailing date, Flt-Lt Evans, sailing officer at RAF Watton, suggested Corporal Russell Brockbank. By the time we had met, we were very short of time for training together – only one Sunday afternoon together, and one full Sunday for Russell to take *Wanderer* off on his own – while I cleared all my office work, and to do this I normally worked a seven-day week before my annual holiday.

I felt that Russell was tough. He had no experience of cruising and little realisation of the shocking conditions of exposure, tiredness and exhaustion, and did not yet fully understand the dangers of a lee shore, but he was a very good helmsman, adaptable and with a sense of humour. I insisted that Russell tell his parents about the cruise and get their agreement, which was readily forthcoming. I found out later that he said he was going on a holiday to Iceland for two weeks, but had been careful not to mention the size of the boat and his parents said they somehow got the impression that it was quite a big boat, probably about 12,000 tons!

My good friends John Galloway and Norman Meekings had co-driven us to our departure points on all previous trips, and had agreed to do so again, returning home with the car and trailer.

In late July we arrived at Kinlochbervie. The fishermen suggested that we launched the dinghy over the beach, below the Hotel Garbet, but the beach was made up of large pebbles, so instead we drove the trailer through a gateway, ignoring a sign 'Beware Dangerous Bull', and launched over the beach. An excellent lunch at the hotel was frequently interrupted by newspaper reporters, who for some reason thought they had a suicide bid on their hands. I listened to the forecast – southerly, Force 5, increasing to 6 by evening, and Force 7 next morning; ideal for making a quick offing from the coast, but a little too rough for the start of a cruise.

The hotel staff were very friendly and I would have given anything to spend the next two weeks where I was. I was suffering very badly from 'cold feet'. It was the hardest cruise I had ever attempted, and Russell as yet had little idea of how extreme conditions might become. *Wanderer* was stowed. Navigation equipment, food in rucksacks, clothes doublewrapped in plastic bags, fruit in plastic buckets. A double check list of the mountainous gear, charts, pilot books, and presents. Petrol stove, swinging oven, and bottles of petrol, and water – all lashed down. The canvas storm cover was fitted on the wash boards of the dinghy. My friends Norman Meekings and John Galloway tried to persuade me to change by the water's edge, but fortunately I realised the reason for their merriment – the hotel staff had said they would be watching us closely through binoculars! I was called to the telephone again, this time by the Wick coastguards. Heaven knows how they heard about our cruise, but they were not too happy about it. I told them I had had some experience offshore, and would send them a postcard on arrival in Iceland. They gave me a forecast – southerly Force 4–5 increasing to 6, dropping tonight but increasing to 7 in Bailey tomorrow.

We cast off at 1645 on 29 July with many waves from the local fishermen, who had been most helpful and regarded our trip as quite normal. I was fearfully nervous and suffering really badly. We beat down the loch due south and turned towards the sea. John Galloway, anticipating conditions on the open sea, had turned down three rolls

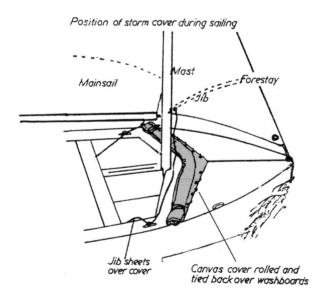

Storm cover rolled up for normal weather.

26

in the mainsail when he had rigged *Wanderer*, but it was sheltered in the loch and we hoisted full sail to enable us to gain ground against a big swell running in. From a hilltop overlooking the loch people were waving to us, and two trawlers ran down to wish us good luck. Wind increased as we reached the open sea, so we turned down a reef above the lower batten. Russell had difficulty removing the batten from its pocket, but he soon got the knack. I turned in at 1830 and asked Russell to call me an hour later so that I could write up the log and watch the land disappear.

Soon there was little wind, so we shook out the reef and put up the jib. An hour later the wind returned, so we reefed again. At 2100 I took over the boat. The wind was southerly Force 5 and 1 hour later it became Force 6, so I hove to and put in a deep reef. We then travelled much easier, going very fast with *Wanderer* rolling heavily as she swept down into a trough and drove through the next crest in a smother of foam. The self-bailer was working very well; it was a newly fitted Elvsrom bailer and, travelling fast, as we were, the water was sucked out of the bilges rapidly. At midnight we changed over. I was very tired, for steering had been difficult with no stars, or even clouds, to steer on. At 0200 I took over again. The wind was still

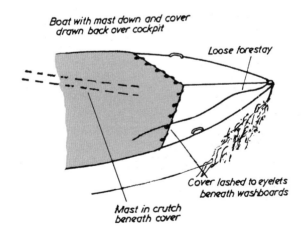

Storm cover drawn over, mast down.

27

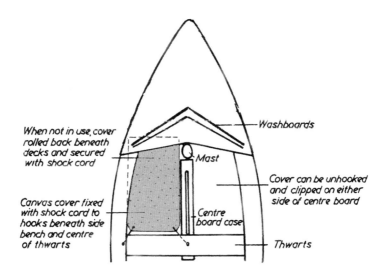

When not in use, cover rolled back beneath decks and secured with shock cord

Washboards

Mast

Cover can be unhooked and clipped on either side of centre board

Canvas cover fixed with shock cord to hooks beneath side bench and centre of thwarts

Centre board case

Thwarts

Headcover, made of waxed canvas. 'Nobody can sleep with water on his face.'

strong and at 0400 I turned in for 3 hours, trying to settle into our normal watches of 2 hours at night and 3 hours during daylight hours.

Russell was sick most of his watch, but later reported that 'it was easy, provided one timed the sickness to the roll of the dinghy'. Otherwise he said 'he got it all back!'

We prepared for the 0630 forecast on 30 July, but we could get no signal from our Homer/Heron DF set. I fitted new batteries and we tried a wire aerial coupled to the shrouds, but we still got no reaction. I cleaned all the contacts and we tried again with no success. The radio had given me no trouble for four years – it was a good set, ideal for open boat work – and I was mystified. Navigation was going to be difficult with no radio DF position and no time signal to check my watch against. I had rated my wrist watch before we left but it was not sufficiently accurate for astronavigation over a two-week period for sun sights. Noon sights would give us our latitude but we must, basically, rely on dead reckoning. The seas were running very big and there were decisions to be made.

2

Dead Reckoning

At 0700 hours Russell was very tired, but just as I got out the stove to heat breakfast, the wind increased to Force 7, so we removed the sails, dropped the mast into the crutch, removed the rudder and laid out the drogue. The seas were 17ft (5.18m) high and breaking heavily. We were uncomfortable and cold. I heated a tin of self-heating soup, which was not much of a breakfast for two men but more than we could manage without being sick. We lay to a drogue for 12 hours,

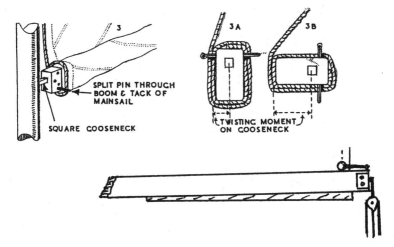

The square gooseneck has been the reefing system on Wanderer *for many years. It is reliable, trouble free and will cope with salt sand and abuse. Care is necessary not to let the boom slip as the split pin can cause injury if the half-reefed sail unrolls out of control.*

The reefing wedge, screwed to the underside of the boom, takes up the extra length of mainsail luff and prevents the heel of the boom dropping when reefed. It is easily removed for class racing.

sodden with sweat and unable to get working. We heard a sound of aircraft engines, which caused Russell to surface.

The Minch specialised in short breaking seas, and the constant motion was tiring. One always started a cruise tired and irritable from the rush of leaving work, and inadequate time for fitting out in detail, but when Russell enquired how far we were from land, I assumed he meant from Scotland and snapped 'About 50 miles'. 'Well,' he said, equally shortly, 'there is an island about 8 miles to leeward!'

This surprised me; as far as I knew, there was no land to the north except the Faeroes and Iceland, and both were several hundred miles beyond the horizon. I grabbed our chart and worked out the reckoning and decided that it must be Sula-Sgeir, a barren and uninhabited rock about ½ mile (800.05m) long and 200yd (182.88m) wide. I had been incredibly slack with my navigation, completely overlooking Sula-Sgeir and its larger neighbour North Rona, when planning the cruise. It needed this kind of shock to make me stop taking risks at sea.

I marked up the passage chart, then we discussed the dangers and difficulties caused by the radio failure. There were three possible alternatives:

1 Iceland – very tricky, with no radio time checks as my watch was not accurate enough to get reliable sights. We would have to dead reckon with noon latitudes for a check; also we could get no weather forecasts when closing the coast and no fix from the coastal radio beacons.
2 Faeroes – more sensible. It was about 200 miles (320km) to Trandisvaag, where we might get the radio repaired. Also it was a much safer landfall, as we could run into the lee of the Faeroes whichever way the wind blew.
3 Run back to Scotland for radio repairs. Unthinkable!

We decided to continue to Iceland. I did not think that Russell had sufficient idea of the high standard of navigation required, nor the problems of getting safely into a dangerous lee shore without a weather forecast, or the general nastiness of having to claw off the coast if caught by an onshore gale, but I decided coldbloodedly that my navigation was adequate and that my fear of a lee shore would

Bad weather early on gives neither of us the chance of settling down to a cruising routine. Lack of sleep was beginning to tell on Russell coming on watch.

serve us well. So I let the decision stand, knowing that the responsibility was mine alone.

We put the mast up at 1900 hours and hoisted the main deep-reefed. The seas were still big, and with the centreboard half raised we were planing fast across them. I promised Russell that I would get some hot food ready at change of watch, but the effort required seemed tremendous. At 2015 I got out the stove and mess tins to heat soup and Irish stew, but found the sea conditions the worst I had ever tried to cook in. The seas were increasing again. Hove to, we just finished eating before the wind increased from Force 6 to 7. So for the second time that day we were forced to take down the mast and lay out a drogue. It was unfortunate that we had encountered two gales in two consecutive days, as we had no chance to settle easily into a system of watches, and consequently we were becoming unnecessarily tired. We had expected two gales in a ten-day crossing, not two gales in the first two days!

By dawn on 31 July the wind had died to south-west Force 2. We felt very cold and damp. One-piece oilskins do keep the water out very well, but we seemed to be just as wet, owing to condensation. We both stripped off to air our many layers of clothes. With a large swell and little wind, the boom was slashing from side to side, and after being struck on the head twice, I tied the murderous thing down to the jib sheet fairlead. This cure was effective for about ten seconds, until the fairlead pulled out of the deck. The fairlead screws were bent and the wood was soft, but we had spare screws in the parts box and used matchsticks to plug the holes. It was a flat calm sea with swells 8–10ft (2.44–3.05m) high, and not too difficult to work in. Towards evening heavy black thunder clouds sat all round our horizon and many squalls raced across the water, but we were clear of them. Gradually the wind backed to NNE and slowly increased to Force 5. Soon we were planing along under reefed main.

The gulls put on a fascinating flying display, swooping down into the troughs and hovering over the crests, never more than two inches above the water. A solan goose – a big white bird with a large wing span, pointed tail and black wing tips – excelled them all. Then the puffins began their antics. They looked just like fat clowns, with rapid wing beats that kept them out of trouble during their circuits and bumps round the dinghy, though they occasionally stalled and crash-landed into the waves in a smother of foam. These birds, with their over-large hooked beaks and eye patches and expression of perpetual surprise, kept us amused for a long time. During the night the wind remained NNE and very squally, and the helmsman was constantly shaking out reefs and putting them in again. We averaged 4 knots all night.

On 1 August, our fourth day at sea, we were still doing 4 knots, but 300° magnetic was the best I could lay. We needed to point higher than this if we were to avoid beating forever. I seemed to be always sailing uphill into a black void and getting nowhere. Russell said that he had not made up his mind whether or not he was enjoying the cruise, and I said that I had made mine up and the answer was 'No'. I put off heating breakfast until the beginning of my next watch, as I was tired

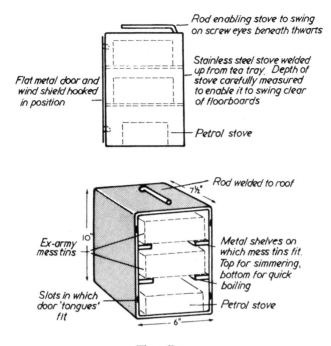

Rod enabling stove to swing on screw eyes beneath thwarts

Stainless steel stove welded up from tea tray. Depth of stove carefully measured to enable it to swing clear of floorboards

Flat metal door and wind shield hooked in position

Petrol stove

Rod welded to roof

7½"

Ex-army mess tins

10"

Metal shelves on which mess tins fit. Top for simmering, bottom for quick boiling

Slots in which door 'tongues' fit

Petrol stove

6"

The galley.

and badly needed sleep. At 1000 the sun came out – marvellous! It inspired us to cook a breakfast of mushroom soup and boiled eggs. It was then that I discovered that Russell did not like boiled eggs much, and he looked glum when I told him we had three dozen aboard. When he wrote up his log, he asked me how to spell 'superb'. He was describing the midnight cup of self-heating cocoa! Our galley, consisting of my home-welded stainless steel gimballed oven containing two mess tins and a petrol Optimus stove, had been much improved since last year, the oven temperature raised and the fuel tank temperature lowered by modifying the air vents. The insulated mugs from which we ate all our food were a tremendous improvement, keeping food much hotter than the plastic mugs we used to carry.

After the meal I worked out the DR position, allowing for a daily drift of 9 miles (14.48km) due to the Gulf Stream, and marked it on the chart. We were still only 130 miles (209.21km) out with 500 miles (804.65km) to go, well below our planned average, owing to the two

Frank working out the estimated position with the chart spread out on the stern buoyancy with Wanderer *hove-to. Navigation was by dead reckoning because the direction finding radio was out of action due to a faulty battery.*

gales and the head winds. We had used about ¾ gallon (3.41 litres) of water, so our estimate of water consumption was about right. The northerly winds would allow us a safe landing on the Vestmann Islands, but we had to guard against being set down the coast and being drawn into the race off Portland. We were sailing close-hauled on 290°, and the wind was northerly, Force 4. I did not resent the northerly wind, because I thought a gale from the north was unlikely during the summer months, and we were working to the west of our course and therefore upwind of Iceland.

I had hoped that we might meet a trawler close to the south coast of Iceland, to get an accurate position before dead reckoning into the coast, but thought that was unlikely as most trawlers would be after herring well north of Iceland at this time of year. So our lives depended on the accuracy of my navigation; I felt the weight of responsibility, but a cold-blooded reappraisal left me still confident that I could do this. Even so, I admit losing a great deal of valuable sleeping time in my off-watch worrying about the problem of navigation and lee shores.

I was suddenly wakened by screams of rage from above. A small seagull was attacking our Norwich Frostbite Sailing Club burgee – going hammer and tongs into the attack with feet and beak. The bird had been hovering in the updraught of our mainsail, and the burgee had slapped him across the head.

Russell said a trawler had crossed our bows during first watch, but he had been unable to switch on the bow navigation lights, so we cleaned the battery contacts and generously greased them with butter. Russell looked tired and cold as he finished his watch. Our clothes were wet through with sweat and condensation. We would change them on Sunday in two days' time. By 1000 it was a flat calm with brilliant sunshine. I photographed Russell as he dried out, oilskins off and top woollens airing, and then took a series of sun sights. The *Air Navigation Tables* greatly simplify the mathematics, and handling the sextant was easy in the calm weather. I took a latitude sight at noon. I had never worked out a noon sight before, but thought, once the sun's declination had been established, it should be simple. The noon position put us 180 miles (289.67km) from Scotland, 350 miles (563.25km) from Iceland, and 50 miles (80.46km) off our proper track.

Position   N 59° 45'
　　　　　　 W 10° 30'

We both had a lazy day, enjoying no wind and soaking in bright sunshine.

Noon Sight

Max Obs Alt		47°	47'
			−2'
		47°	45'
Declination		42°	15'
		17°	53'
		60°	8'

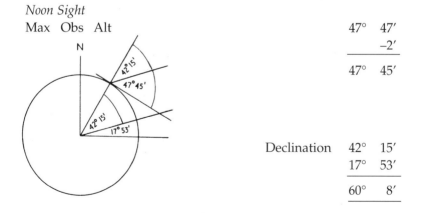

We had a washing-up session, cleaning everything in sight – mess tins, stove, cutlery, tin opener, ourselves. I felt happier. This had been a welcome day's rest; I was not quite so worried about the lack of radio, because we could get such good fixes with the sextant. I was very glad that I had bought one after all.

We had now settled into a definite routine. We were in good physical shape and had hardened up. Our clothing had dried out and been aired in the sun, except for Russell's tracksuit, which was still rather 'high'.

After tea we took another set of sun sights, and I plotted them against the morning and noon sights. These gave us an amazing 'cocked hat' of only 6 miles (9.66km) long by 3 miles (4.83km) wide. I now assumed our position had been established at 60° 10′ N, 11° W (obviously this position was dependent on the accuracy of my watch, but the noon sight I knew to be accurate and all three seemed to tie up well). Only 300 miles (482.79km) to Iceland, and so we sorted out the coastal charts and folded them ready.

Two gulls had been swimming alongside all afternoon, and we threw them the peel of an orange. Immediately they were joined by ten others, who fought for the spoils. Having decided on the winner, they found they did not like the orange peel anyway, and left it in disgust.

It was a lovely calm summer evening, and we sat chatting idly until Russell turned in at 2000 hours, alongside the centreboard. There was a breath of wind from the south west at 2045 and within 15 minutes *Wanderer* was planing hard. Then, as I hove to, in order to reef, the wind died to a flat calm again.

The sunset was spectacular. The sun fell into the sea, and suddenly the sky was lit red and lurid from below the horizon. Round the northern sky tremendous banks of clouds built up, starting at 10,000ft (3,048m) and rising to 50,000ft (15,240m). They looked like mauve hills and massive valleys rising to gigantic mountain ranges. I let my mind range free, enjoying the fantastic eerie sight. In the centre was a cloud shaped like a wolf's head. Twisting round to the east, I went rigid with fear – jumping down at us from a cloud mountain top was a wolf, saliva dripping from his jaws, his toes spread to land on the boat, and his eyes blazing in the sun's rays. One

Fifth day at sea. Russell eats bread and cheese for lunch. Now we had settled down into a cruising routine and this was one of the few days we could relax.

of Hel's hounds! God! I really believed him to be there. Even now I can remember sitting there, petrified, staring at that frightening sight. I must have remained like that for 30 seconds before I was able to wrench my mind back to reality, to find that I was trembling like a leaf and running with sweat.

I thought then how easy it was to understand the old Norse belief that Vikings killed in battle went to Valhalla, where they spent their time feasting and fighting; but those who died of old age or illness were sent to the goddess Hel, who each day fed them to her two pet wolves, so that they spent eternity in agony.

3

Force Eight

When I came on duty at 0130 hours on 2 August, we were planing fast, there were stars to steer by, and our speed was 6–7 knots in winds of 4 plus. By the end of my watch I had reefed twice and the wind was a strong Force 5. When we changed watch, I warned Russell about holding on to sail too long and of the dangers of a broach. Russell called me urgently at 0400; he had reefed right down to the third batten, and still *Wanderer* was overpowered and he wanted to down sail and lay to the drogue. However, although the seas were 10–12ft (3.05–3.66m), *Wanderer* was lifting easily, but she was running too fast and pulling the crests down on her; so we lowered the mainsail and carried on broad reaching under the genoa only. I shortened watches to one hour each, which was as long as the helmsman could concentrate in these conditions.

Gradually the wind built up to a southerly Force 7, with seas running 15ft (4.57m) high, but luckily heavy rain beat the seas down. Our new Whale bilge pump was a big improvement, with a greater capacity and easier action than its predecessor, but the intake filter did occasionally need cleaning. When I had fitted it, I never expected to be lifting the floorboards in a Force 7 in the middle of the North Atlantic. Russell watched me with suspicion but without comment – good man! The filter gauze was blocked with fluff, raisins and matchsticks.

By 1100 the seas were running level with the mast head, and waves were occasionally breaking in spite of the heavy rain, hitting the side of the hull with a tremendous crash and surrounding us in a cascade of foam; but, with the centreboard half raised, *Wanderer* was able to slip safely sideways. Russell looked a little scared, but I explained that only waves that break downwards were dangerous.

A radio forecast would have been nice. I thought that it looked like blowing even harder, but I would like to have been told so officially.

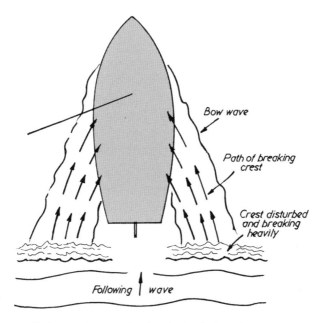

Bow wave

Path of breaking crest

Crest disturbed and breaking heavily

Following | wave

Waves do not climb over the stern but break alongside and come aboard over the beam. I could not understand why until I realised that it is the bow wave that disturbs the following crest, causing it to break alongside in a mass of foam and come aboard just aft of the shrouds.

Wanderer began to roll heavily, so we dropped the jib, removed the rudder and lay to the drogue. I had gone forward many times to unshackle the jib, but never in worse conditions. Waves were breaking heavily, and the varnished deck was very slippery, with water flooding over the bows several inches deep. There was little to hold on to as the bows dropped sickeningly as each crest passed under the boat, and I was glad of my life line. We waited for a calm patch and then lowered the mast into the crutch and tied down the cover. Had we left this 10 minutes longer, we should have been in real trouble, because a series of the heaviest breaking seas I had yet seen roared by. They did us no damage, but had we still been sailing, they would certainly have capsized us. It always surprised me how comfortably a dinghy rode to a drogue. Beneath the storm cover it was difficult to tell that a gale was blowing; only the hiss of the breaking crest and the bang as it hit the hull, the rattle of spray on the cover, the quick jump of the boat as she gave way to the wave, and the warning whine of the wind reminded one of the conditions only a few inches away.

It was warm under the cover and we slept deeply, well satisfied with the 60 miles (96.56km) we had travelled since yesterday.

For the next 20 hours we lay to the drogue, with hourly inspections for shipping, and slept. We heated soup twice but had difficulty keeping it down. According to the chart, we were on the Outer Bailey Banks – no wonder the seas were heavy! (They were also given their alternative name of Lousy Banks on the chart.)

On Sunday, 4 August, at 0300 hours the gale was still blowing Force 8 from the south. The floorboards had become very hard, and we were cold and tired of the whining wind. By 0830 the seas had died down sufficiently to remove the cover, raise the mast and hoist the mainsail reefed. It was pleasant to be sailing again, worth all the mental effort of getting going. With the wind backed into the south east, broad reaching at 6 knots and the sun out, we felt warmed and happier. Russell did not like the possibility of a gybe, and so was steering high. I explained that accurate steering was all important as we were dead reckoning, but did not add that our lives depended on good navigation.

At noon I took a sextant sight. *Wanderer* was planing very fast on a broad reach, it was rather rough and difficult to obtain an accurate sight in a big seaway. I found it very difficult to hold the sextant steady on the horizon; with one's shoulder against the mast the sextant vibrated. I found the only way was to keep the body supported below the waist, leaving the upper half free to flex with the boat movement. Taking the last sight for cross bearing against this noon sight, I marked up our position on the chart by a transfer position line. It was a wonderful few hours' sail – broad reaching at 6 knots in brilliant sunshine.

That evening watch was the hardest of the cruise. It was a cold and miserable night and we were close-hauled. There were thunder clouds everywhere and squalls kept whistling out of a pitch black night. I had to pump out twice during the squalls, over 100 strokes each time. It seemed just like a nightmare, continually reefing to meet a squall, sitting out until it had passed, then shaking out the reefs, pumping out, and then reefing again as *Wanderer* was overpowered by another squall. After 2 hours of that it seemed that wherever I pointed the dinghy there in the darkness was a squall waiting to pounce. With head winds our course was only N20°W and our speed 2 knots. I was only too thankful when my watch ended and I could turn the responsibility over to Russell.

So we carried on, and two days later at 2000 the marked-up chart read 62°N, 17° 30'W. The nearest land was only 90 miles (144.21km) direct, with Gardhskagi Cape 200 miles (321.86km) away and Vestmannaeyjar 120 miles (193.12km). Sights and DR agreed closely.

I noticed Russell shaking badly an hour later, and insisted that we both changed completely. I lugged all our spare clothes from the front buoyancy and we started to strip. It was cold in bare skin in a Force 6 this far north, but a brisk towelling was relaxing and dry clothes wonderful. It was a long job but well worth it. *Wanderer* looked a shambles. The wet (and stinking) clothes were stowed forward, and the merely damp ones put in the stern buoyancy. Russell looked slightly better, but still pretty dreadful – a yellow face pinched with cold and coal black bags under his eyes. I probably looked just as bad as he, but luckily we had no mirror. We badly needed hot food. Thank heavens for our swinging stove, making it possible, even in bad conditions, to have nourishing food! Russell kept fiddling with his hot food until it cooled, which annoyed me, after I had troubled to make it. He said he had a tender mouth, but I told him it was better to suffer a burnt tongue than lose the benefit from the hot meal. It was another black night, rough and very squally.

On Tuesday, 6 August, the wind was still westerly, Force 6, with big head seas, and it was cold and rough. In such short seas with a strong head wind we were doing little more than holding our own, and several times we considered lying to a drogue, but held on to our sail reefing and unreefing for the squalls. Our efficiency was deteriorating through lack of proper sleep and insufficient food. We must eat more often. During my watch from 0300 to 0600 hours there were black line squalls all round the horizon. *Wanderer* was already deep-reefed but I removed the third batten in case I needed another reef. I could hear the squalls moving all round us in the darkness, but fortunately all passed clear of us. It was a wearing experience, though.

It was a spectacular dawn. The sky was a fantastic dome of pink and orange all round the horizon, especially to the north east and south, and it seemed to rise upwards for mile after mile. I took some photographs because nobody would have believed such a sight.

We decided in future to cook at least two hot meals a day, and use our self-heating tins on the early watches. Russell tried our radio set and, surprisingly, got weak signals from a radio beacon. They were faint, but we got Harnafjordur bearing 30° (magnetic) and Vestmannaeyjar 315°. It was a great relief to get a fix, although we treated it as suspect. Later the weather cleared and it became a beautiful clear sunny day, winds Force 2, and we cooked a really big meal. I fell asleep off watch, for the first time completely warm and well fed, and slept deeply. Russell called me urgently half an hour later to say the starboard rigging screw had broken! I felt dreadful, having just dropped into a deep sleep, and it took some minutes for the message to get through to me. Fortunately he had tacked immediately to transfer the weight to the other shroud, although this too had been bent in one of the gales. It was very lucky that it had not parted during the vicious weather on the outer Bailey Bank, and it was also fortunate that, as a result of losing our mast a year earlier owing to a broken rigging screw, I had fitted safety lashings to the shrouds. I fitted shackles to the shroud plates and then replaced the rigging screws with terylene lashings. I was completely exhausted after the repair, but was too tired to sleep, so took advantage of the good weather to check our food supplies. This removed one of my worries, for we had sufficient water for ten days, food for six days, and cooker fuel for two weeks.

4

Land

During the late afternoon the clouds lifted to show the land. What a wonderful sight it was! The coastline was invisible below the horizon, but there was the tremendous glacier Eyjafjalla and the volcano Hekla just above the horizon, still 100 miles (160.93km) away. I kicked Russell awake in great excitement and shouted 'Land'. The result was disappointing: he just said 'Oh' and went back to sleep.

The compass bearings on Portland, Hekla and Eyjafjalla did not agree with our DR position, but on checking back I discovered that I had made a mistake in calculating the magnetic variation (the magnetic variation alters very quickly when approaching Iceland and I had allowed 32°, whereas it was only 22°). If the wind held true, we could round Portland next day.

Soon it began blowing up rapidly from the north east. Immediately *Wanderer* lifted up on to a plane. I held on to full sail as long as I could, but eventually reefed to the lower batten, and removed the second batten in case further reefs became necessary.

Wanderer was going like an express train when I came back on watch at 0100 on Wednesday, 8 August – 8 knots on a fine reach, bows lifted clear of the water, and a plume of spray trailing astern from the rudder. Russell had his feet under the toe straps and was sitting right out and said we had been going like that for 2 hours. 'Wonderful sailing,' he yelled. 'This is what I came for.'

Back on watch I pulled in the jib a little and we really began to move. It was difficult to steer in the dull black darkness before dawn – so dark that I could not even see the silhouette of the mainsail above me, so I steered on the sound of the jib. It was difficult to find anything else to steer on with no stars, no moon and no clouds – and our compass is unlit. I adjusted the jib so that it was drawing on course and flapping immediately *Wanderer* luffed up. To check I was

Russell taking an RDF bearing near Iceland.

on course I occasionally luffed until I heard the jib flap and paid off again. I called it 'steering by ear', and told Russell I was deeply impressed with my ingenuity. I gathered he was not! We did not come off the plane. Marvellous sailing – the exhilaration that one remembered long after the cold and the discomfort had been forgotten. Russell's next watch was also spent planing at 8 knots and the seas were big. By mid-morning the overcast sky had given way to brilliant sunshine, and the wind had swung into the south west, Force 1 and the sea had died down. We spread out our sodden clothing to dry; until the boat was covered with it.

A further weak radio fix put us considerably to the east of Portland – obviously the *Pilot* was correct when mentioning a strong current to eastwards along the coast off Portland. It seemed that we had been set 25 miles (40.23km) eastwards that day.

Several fishing boats were visible on the horizon, and late that afternoon we beat up to the Norwegian trawler *Vestliner*. It seemed to take hours to come up with her, beating into the light and fickle wind. I was on tenterhooks lest she finished hauling her lines and steamed off before we could get our position and a weather forecast, for we were already too close to the coast to be safe if the weather turned nasty. They had been long lining for cod. Their line was a steel cable with a cod hook every 20ft (6.10m). We noticed that every hook was taken and large cod were brought aboard every 15 seconds. One man winched in the line and killed the fish by hitting it on the head and knocking it into the water, a second man hooked it aboard and the third man gutted it. They worked extremely fast.

The skipper did not speak English, so we held out our chart and drew a large question mark in the air above it with a forefinger, and looked at our watches in amazement. He dashed into the bridgehouse while the crew fended off our spreaders from the superstructure. He passed a piece of paper to us and this showed that our watches had gained considerably. The skipper's Decca position agreed closely with our radio fix – 15.40 BSS, 63° 19'N, 17° 44'W. The position was within 7 miles (11.27km) of our last radio fix. Allowing for distortion of radio from Vestmannaeyjar crossing land, and the distance sailed in the last 1 hour 40 minutes, the error was only 3 miles (4.83km). The Homer/Heron set is excellent, even on reduced power. The skipper was unable to give us a weather forecast, but thought that another depression was approaching our area. With many shouts of '*Lykke til*' following us, we sailed away.

The wind remained very light south-westerly, which was frustrating, for we needed a steady wind to close the land. We were much too close to it to be safe, and I felt extremely uneasy. With a good wind, we could be ashore next day. We had been at sea for nine days and our equipment was suffering: Russell's camera had seized up, the charts and navigation tables had become damp and difficult to use, the dividers had seized with salt corrosion and, worst of all, said Russell, his pencil had split from top to bottom. As it bore the legend 'with the compliments of Eileen Ramsay, marine photographer', he had naturally assumed when he stole it that it was a seagoing pencil, and he was badly shaken to find that the glue was soluble. As he pointed out, 'You can't trust anyone these days!'

Myrdal glacier had been visible for some time and now we saw Portland for the first time. The detached mountain to seaward of the glacier had to be Portland (it might even be the Vestmann Islands if the visibility was exceptional). Myrdal glacier was a wonderful sight, for we could see peak after peak of glacial ice.

Just before midnight the wind veered to WNW, heading us again, and I swore viciously. Beating into the wind in daylight is difficult enough, but to do it in the dark off a strange lee shore is asking for trouble. I thought about the problem and decided to stand in towards the coast on the port tack for 2 hours, then come about at each change of watch. At least it would simplify the dead reckoning and at dawn we should be near enough to identify the coast. That was an error.

Russell handed over to me at 0030. The wind was right in our teeth, Force 4–5, and he had reefed to the lower batten. I picked up Portland light (by dawn, after a long hard thrash to windward on the port tack, it was behind our beam). One hour later we ran into heavy overfalls. We were carried into this tide race with barely a warning. Suddenly I heard the roar of breaking seas, and then the frightening sight of 18ft (5.49m) waves looming up out of the darkness and breaking in all directions. Lumps of water seemed to rise straight out of the sea, churning and breaking in all directions from that white cauldron of water. Seas were roaring and hissing all around us. Sometimes they broke beneath us, at other times alongside and sometimes downwards on top of us. *Wanderer* went up some of them, and at other times she would slide down into a trough and the water would collapse on to her in a roaring mass of foam. I tacked immediately, but the wind was light and it took another 20 minutes to work clear of that most dangerous area. Once clear, I found that I was sweating badly. Amazingly, Russell was still asleep, and I did not wake him as there was little he could have done, and probably it was more frightening than dangerous. Pumping out took a considerable time.

On Thursday, 8 August, during my first watch, the head wind increased to Force 6. Suddenly the wind died to Force 2, and we were wrapped in thick fog, with visibility of only 80yd (73.15m) and no wind. Only 25 miles (40.23km) to go! I asked Russell to pass me the foghorn, as a precaution, but he was sound asleep so I took pity on him and did not wake him. We were well away from shipping lanes anyhow. I was getting worried about Russell, as he was looking dreadful and beginning to suffer from exhaustion. I hoped he was not relying on getting ashore that day, for nothing is certain at sea and such a disappointment would come as a shock. I tried to warn him against this as he took the dawn watch. I don't think he realised how hard he had been working, or how fatigue and the extreme conditions had sapped his endurance. At 0600 hours the sun burnt up the fog. Russell still looked dreadful, and as I went below I told him to call me if he needed me.

It was difficult to relax so close to the shore, but I must have slept, because at 0800 I woke suddenly as I heard the whine of wind in the rigging. God, how I hated that sound! *Wanderer* was heeling, waves were crashing against the weather chine only two inches from my face. Another gale! Blast the weather! Damn and blast! This would mean two more days at sea.

5

Collapse

I shouted encouragement to Russell – probably fatuous in the circumstances – but got no reply. I shouted again – still no reply! I tore off the head cover thinking that he might have gone overboard and with great relief saw him. He sat at the tiller, the picture of dejection, completely exhausted. Tears rolling down his face, he said, 'Frank, I have reefed twice and she needs another one but I can't do it.' He had backed the jib, but could not summon the energy to complete the job. He looked longingly at the shore only 15 miles (24.14km) away, completely at the end of his tether. He had worked himself to a standstill, and the knowledge that we had to ride out another gale so near the shore had destroyed his morale. I knew just how he felt because on an earlier cruise, in fact only my second one, during a gale

Under the cover it was difficult to realise that a gale was blowing outside. Wanderer *was riding well with a slight snatch as the drogue pulled her over each breaking crest, a rattle of spray on the cover, and an occasional jump sideways as a cross sea caught her.* Winston Megoran.

Chartwork on a dinghy can be challenging.

off Heligoland, I had suffered similar exhaustion and collapse – a shattering experience and only the greater stamina and experience of my crew John Buckingham had pulled us through. As a result, the sailor becomes a better seaman, and he suddenly develops a wholesome respect for the sea.

I sent Russell below and helped him into his berth alongside the centreboard case. I would have to get him ashore as soon as possible. I was really worried about him now. I set about lowering the jib and reefing the main – jolly tricky in the present sea, as we had left it too late. Large seas were now breaking. Vestmannaeyjar was up to windward 25 miles (40.23km). We could make it if the wind eased, but it was hopeless with seas building up.

I considered tacking and reaching in to the coast, for it would have eased my mind to get a doctor to Russell. I dismissed the idea as quite impractical. East of Portland the *Pilot* said landing was possible only in ideal conditions and with wind setting along the coast, big seas and tricky overfalls could be expected.

By 0930 conditions for headway were impossible, owing to large breaking seas. I decided to lay to a drogue, and told Russell to stay below while I lowered jib and main, and paid out the drogue. I would hate to have to sew up a torn ear as well, so shouted to Russell to keep clear of the handle of the warp drum as it rotated as the warp went out. I tied the warp round the thwart, and lowered the mast into the crutch. I delayed tying down the cockpit cover as I hoped the gale would blow out quickly, but instead draped it around Russell for extra warmth. We both needed hot food, so I heated a can of self-heating soup, but forgot to pierce the can. I expected it to explode, and would almost have been grateful for the extra warmth but was too tired even to anticipate the possibility of a burn if it spurted over my hand when I pierced it.

A trawler passed ¾ mile (1.21km) to starboard, and I suggested to Russell that I put him aboard and brought *Wanderer* in later. He said a very firm 'No', which pleased me enormously, as I would have had to put up a red flare to attract attention, and that might have brought out a lifeboat from the coast, a dreadfully unnecessary and humiliating operation. After a meal Russell said he felt warmer.

Suddenly *Wanderer* began to drift fast and sheer about – the drogue warp must have chafed through. Fortunately it had only tied itself in knots and was soon sorted out. After taking bearings on the mountains, I could see that we were drifting eastwards at about 2 knots, losing all our hard-won ground, so I decided to sail again in the afternoon if Russell could stand a watch, for the wind was dropping to Force 6. The drogue tied itself in a ball twice more; it seems that below Force 7 the parachute drogue collapses as the pull decreases.

By tea time the seas were still too bad for sailing, so I heated soup and Irish stew, and decided to lay to a drogue all night. I turned in but was much too tired to sleep. During the evening the seas became easier so we set off again with small jib and reefed main. Russell took the first watch, still looking tired and exhausted, and I felt rather like he looked. Vestmannaeyjar was dead ahead – we had head winds, head seas, and were just laying 260°, and the boat was pounding heavily into the short steep seas. Our clothes had become very foul and we were both very cold and wet. Our speed fell to 2 knots or less as *Wanderer* slammed heavily down into each trough, so we shook out a reef and later put up full sail to drive her through the chop.

Late that night the coast seemed to fall away to the west of the glacier very slowly to a long low coastline. A little further round on the horizon, right in the eye of the sunset (otherwise I would not have seen it) was a bump on the skyline.

That must be it! We hove to, took a RDF bearing and found it was indeed Vestmannaeyjar bearing 340° magnetic. We tacked, and were almost able to lay it, when the wind fell away completely. After eating, I turned in, and 2 hours later was back on watch, more tired than ever.

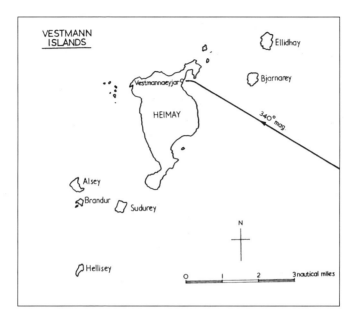

The following morning of 9 August was our eleventh day at sea and there was very little wind. Just before dawn I saw a white light, and then the red and green sector light appeared as well. It was not possible to count the flashes accurately because they kept disappearing behind swells. It was nevertheless pleasant to know that we were so close to land and I sailed on towards them. Blast! As daylight came, I realised those lights belonged to a trawler, but she was on the right bearing!

It was no good sailing without wind, so I hove to in discouragement and turned in on the floorboards, using a gallon tin of oil as a pillow. I did not call Russell, for *Wanderer* would look after herself for a bit. It was bitterly cold, far too cold to sleep. My trousers were saturated with sweat and condensation – they felt very clammy and high. Both Russell and I were now in quite a low state.

At 0750 there was a light wind from the north east, just enough to give steerage way. Russell sailed, and I turned in. I was shivering violently and my feet felt like blocks of ice. Though I was afraid to move in case they fell off, I got up and walked around the dinghy for warmth and exercise. Two strides down the floorboards, and two back. By 1100 the Vestmann Islands were clear above the horizon, the nicest land we had seen for a long time. As it was a fine sunny day, we stripped off to dry. My fingernails were very painful, with salt driven deep beneath their edges, and the insides of my fingers and thumbs were covered in cracks, inflamed and raw. It made writing the log very painful and difficult.

The wind was on the beam, light and variable, and I hoped it would not die away for nothing is so frustrating as not being able to move within sight of one's goal. We had breakfast and lunch combined, and as we hoped that would be our last meal at sea, we dug deeply into the stores, enjoying tinned grapefruit and soft boiled eggs mashed in butter.

Russell looked up the sketches of the islands in the *Pilot*. They looked to be seven barren rocks, but the harbour was well hidden, and so was the town of Heimay, the second largest cod port in Iceland. The wind came up ESE, Force 4, and we began to plane on a broad reach. I told Russell we would be ashore in 5 hours, and kept my fingers crossed for the wind to last. It would be depressing to be becalmed 10 miles (16.09km) offshore, and Russell was running out of holiday. In view of his comments about me heaving to unnecessarily, I kept *Wanderer* sailing hard, using the 'heads' and writing up the log while still at the tiller. Within an hour the islands were close enough for us to pick out details.

▲ 1966 Loading *Wanderer* onto a British Rail lorry to be transported back to Norfolk in a railway wagon after a summer cruise in the Orkney and Shetland Islands. The huge advantage of a cruising dinghy is that after a holiday one can get her home in a variety of ways – road transport, railway, deck cargo on a coaster, by ferry or furniture van, or even trailing.

▲ 1963 First night on passage from North Scotland (Kinlockbervie) to Norway via Faeroe Islands. Supper of cold chicken – Frank carving.

1965 Dried out in Uig Bay, west coast of Harris, outer Hebrides, after a fast passage from St Kilda. We ran through the narrow rocky entrance in the dark on a compass bearing and anchored after midnight. Next morning the unexpected view was a wonderful surprise.

▲ 1970 First night's camp, dried out in a rocky bay, Lofoten Islands, Northern Norway – our favourite campsite in 50 years' cruising. The peace and silence was endless.

◀ 1970 Arctic Norway. Margaret preparing supper. Hot food is essential when temperatures drop dramatically at the end of their short summer.

▲ 1970 Margaret studying the Sailing Directions as we approach the first of the maelstrom whirlpools in the fjords of Northern Norway.

▼ 1972 Cove at Aberdaron, North Wales. Overnighting, awaiting the tide around the Lleyn Peninsula, with its fearsome Tripods Race.

▲ 1976 River cruising in Autumn – the upper reaches of the River Dee.

▼ 1978 Stowage in a dinghy has to be highly organised! A break for coffee.

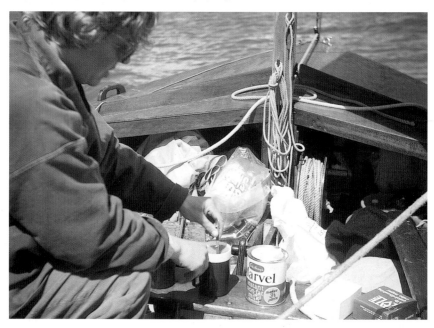

1977 Our re-designed tent (which we christened 'The Hilton'). Sitting headroom throughout the boat is a great luxury.

▲ 1983 Florida. Christmas cruise using the canals and waterways to cross Florida from the Atlantic coast to Lake Okeechobee to the Gulf of Mexico. Frank shaving while Margaret cooks breakfast ashore.

▼ Oct 1988 Singlehanding through New York, end of season. A magnificent skyline but a dangerous place for a dinghy without an engine because of the constant commercial traffic kicking up huge wakes. Freighters, liners, tug boats, barges and ferries do not expect small sailing dinghies in these waters.

▲ 1993 *Wanderer* hauled out in a rocky pool on a 40 mile crossing of Georgian Bay to the Bruce Peninsula. Bad weather approaching. The Great Lakes, Canada.

▼ We hauled out *Wanderer* over rocks using boat rollers and then jammed the anchor in a rocky fissure.

▲ 1998 Locking through the 19th century Trent Severn Waterway system in Canada. These large deep locks are used today for pleasure craft; their size, depth and speed of filling the chamber can cause extreme turbulence for small craft.

▼ Margaret dwarfed by the great mitre gates of a lock on the Trent Severn Waterway.

6

Vestmann Islands

How grim and barren our landfall looked; grass only seemed to grow on the mountain tops. The *Pilot* told us that there was a population of 2,000 and that the entrance to the harbour was invisible until one was close under the cliffs. We looked for a gap between the mountains of the main island. We headed well eastwards of the island, because the tide turned to a west-going stream close in, splitting round the island, and we needed to be in the northern stream to avoid being swept past the islands. The wind was dead astern and the jib stick was rigged, for the first time in the whole trip. We ate our last Enerzade glucose tablets and finished off most of our other bits and pieces of foodstuffs – butter, Ryvita and dates. I checked our remaining stores: we still had sufficient food for four more sea days, and enough water for eight days further, so our estimate for fourteen days at sea was not far wrong. Russell finished his last cigarette. He said it was quite a relief, because they had become so stale and damp that it was a pleasure no longer to have to force himself to smoke them.

I suggested that nothing was certain at sea, and even now an accident could delay us getting ashore, but I did not really believe that myself. There was a complete change in us both. All the tiredness was forgotten, and we were cheerful and joking.

Heimay was only about 3 miles (4.83km) away but it looked smaller than the chart suggested. We could see the houses clearly but the entrance was still invisible. I hoped there would be a hotel ashore, for a good bath and bed were what I longed for.

Russell nearly climbed the mast in anguish because I insisted on taking photographs while sailing between the patches of rocks, just awash, all round the harbour entrance. I was steering with my knee, but it could not have been obvious how hard I was concentrating. We met quite short steep seas while approaching the entrance to the

Wanderer *makes her landfall at the Vestmann Islands off the south coast of Iceland – 11 days and four gales out from Scotland.*

harbour, since the tide and wind together were piling up water into this funnel-like entrance. Removing the jib stick as we approached, we gybed over and reached through the entrance and then put up our red ensign.

We sailed round the harbour, putting our nose into each quay to see if we could locate a comfortable berth. I had learnt from past experience that it was time well spent looking round before tying up. We were hailed several times and asked 'Where from?', and a rapidly increasing crowd followed us along the quays. Russell wanted to tie up to a stone wall, but there would have been too much damage to our rubbing strake, so I decided to tie up by a fishing boat. We luffed up smartly and came alongside the boat's stern beautifully, while Russell jumped on the bows to tie up, quite forgetting that he was still attached to our thwarts by his lifeline. He could not reach by a hand's length and so we drifted slowly away and had to paddle back – with all the fishermen watching, too!

After tying up to the stern of the fishing boat, we climbed on to the quay, and found it very difficult to walk. We had lost our land legs. An Icelandic fisherman, Marteinn Fridjonson, greeted us, and took us to the fish factory to meet a Canadian who could speak English. We asked the latter about the island and if there was a hotel, but he did not like the 'goddam islands, he did not like the goddam hotel, there wasn't a bath in the goddam hotel, the food was lousy and the goddam stuff was uneatable!' Marteinn took us next to the police station to have our passports stamped, but we were told to return in the morning. The local time was 1700 hours.

Walking back to the harbour, we found a customs officer waiting. He drove us up to his office and stamped our papers – there was some confusion over *Wanderer*'s tonnage – and then drove us round to the Hotel HB to book us in for the night.

At the shipping office we discovered that there was a ship for Reykjavik the following day. She was a coastal ship, sailing at 2200 and arriving at Reykjavik the following morning at 0800. Running out of holiday, we booked ourselves and *Wanderer* as deck cargo and returned to the hotel, where we asked for plenty of hot water and had a standup bathe – there were no baths on the island because there was no water supply, and all rain water had to be stored.

In the restaurant we sat down to enjoy the meal. It was superb. Soup, lamb and fish. Halfway through the meal, Russell looked up and said, 'Cor! Look at that! Isn't it gorgeous?' I looked up to see an attractive waitress coming through the door and I watched her walk the length of the room with approval, but when I turned to congratulate Russell on his taste he was referring to the cup of steaming coffee he had just been given – which just shows how eleven days at sea can distort a person's outlook! We walked around the town before turning in, and sent the necessary cables home. The upper end of the town was the cleaner, its concrete houses contrasting strangely with the galvanised buildings of the harbour area.

Telephone calls came in from the UK from 0800 onwards. Brian Fawcett of the BBC remarked that it was a pity we had landed on the Friday night; it would have been much better had we spent the weekend at sea and arrived on the Monday morning, so that the news would have been fresh! Russell worked very hard to get the dinghy ready for shipping, while I was tied up contacting friends and people who had helped us with advice and equipment.

Our fisherman friend joined us, and we gathered that during the wartime occupation he had liked the British, had tolerated the Americans but had disliked the French Canadians. Marteinn's parents had had English soldiers billeted on them on New Year's Eve, so he had dropped a celebration firework down the stove chimney – and out had come the English with bayonets fixed and ready to fight. Everybody, including the troops, had thought it very funny, and the ice had been broken.

I wanted to climb a mountain, but could not persuade Russell to join me, as his feet were in an even worse condition than mine – the result of wet socks and wearing rubber Wellingtons for too long. I decided on the volcano to the east of the island, as it would give me a better view across Heimay. Passing the pretty Lutheran Church, I felt sorry we should not be there on Sunday, as I would have liked to go to church there. It was an easy walk to the top of the grass, and then a tiring climb over loose volcanic ash at the angle of 45°. Needing a rest, I waited and was overtaken by an Icelander and his son, who told me that Iceland was inhabited before the Vikings by a religious sect from Ireland, called 'Papa'. Not much is known about them except that they were Christian. When the Vikings landed, they either left or were slain. I continued my scramble up to the volcanic crater, now at an angle of 60° over loose scree, and eventually I reached the edge of the crater. The scenery from this height was most impressive. The centre of the island was very fertile and well sheltered by the mountains, except to the south, where there was an airstrip and the harbour. Across the 10-mile (16.09-km) sound I could clearly see the grim barren mainland rising to the glaciers and mountains of the interior. During the days of sail the loss of life trying to make harbour in a south-easterly gale must have been enormous.

Having taken my fill of scenery, I scrambled down the scree. Back at the hotel Russell and I had the best vegetable soup I have ever tasted, followed by fish fresher than one usually sees it in England. We were joined by our fisherman friends, who told us that although the previous winter in England was hard, in Iceland it was unusually warm. In fact they said one Englishman came to Iceland in January with an array of Arctic clothing, prepared for a cold reception, and it was so warm that he found that the Icelanders were wearing only their smiles!

Vestmannaeyjar Harbour seen from the top of the volcano.

We were taken to the ship bound for Reykjavik, and introduced to the steward by our friends. We waved goodbye, sorry to leave some beautiful islands, but anxious to see as much as possible of Iceland in the remaining two days. Russell had to start work on the Friday, which meant flying home on the Wednesday, so we still had 48 hours to explore western Iceland.

In Reykjavik Russell retired at the Hotel Gardur to rest his feet, while I hunted out some clean clothes from *Wanderer*'s hold. Returning to the hotel, I met the receptionist, who told me where Russell was, obviously thinking it very funny that men needed to rest their feet. No good comes of keeping them wet and in rubber boots for days on end. Mine also felt too painful to stand for long.

I walked to look up a contact, and spent an afternoon with Mr Johannes Jonsson and his charming wife. We had tea and I enjoyed Icelandic pancakes filled with cream and jam. Then I returned to Russell and put my feet up before they seized.

The following day we took a bus tour to Thingvellir. The scenery was impressive, but did not come up to Norwegian standards. Our guide told us that all active volcanoes were called by girls' names, which I found quite funny, but Russell, who was missing his girlfriend, could not see the humour. We stopped at the hot springs area of Hveragerdi. Several greenhouses in the area were heated by the hot springs, the whole area being honeycombed with them, and with geysers. The hot water was pumped over 50 miles (80.46km) to Reykjavik, where it arrived at 86°C and was used for central heating. A geyser was persuaded to erupt for us – a large lump of soap was dropped into it, and we were told that some types of soap were better than others. Our journey continued through larva fields – weird and fascinating in their loneliness. Great waves of lava 20ft (6.10m) high rolled towards us, moss green in the foreground shading away to bluish-yellow and black, and in the distance the dark purple mountains outlined sharply against the setting sun. Legends of ghosts and phantoms abounded from this area, and it was easy to see why! One legend told of a beautiful lady who begged a lift from a passing motorist and then asked to drive his car. Once behind the wheel, she drove the car into a ravine, and next morning the dead driver was found in the crumbled car, but the beautiful lady had disappeared. Our guide sang us a song of the area to the rhythm of horses' hoofs – obviously a rider was urging his horse to clear the area before darkness fell, before being taken by the trolls and ghosts, and he was singing to keep up his spirits. The song was very moving. Further along we saw rack after rack of cod drying in the air.

During the bus journey I became friendly with Anna, a Norwegian from Oslo. She had sat two rows in front of me but, as I joined her and carried on a conversation, I learnt that she was a medical librarian returning from a study course in the USA. She also wanted to see a little of Iceland before going home. She knew Frederik Thorne, the Norwegian judge whose dining-room floor I once slept on during a previous cruise to Norway. What a small world! Since we could talk about Norway, our holiday friendship grew easily. I saw Anna back to her hotel and then hobbled back to our own. My feet by now were prepared to argue before obeying the command 'walk'.

Tuesday was our last day in Iceland. I had told Anna I would take her for a sail, and the radio and television had asked for interviews, so I went to the docks to rig *Wanderer*. It was a cold miserable day blowing hard from the north west and there was a swell even inside the harbour. I went to collect Anna, at the Hotel Borg, thinking that she would not wish to sail in such cold stormy weather. I was pleased to find, however, that she had been looking forward to it, irrespective of weather. How nice! I wanted a sail, too, and had been thinking how good it would be to have the time to sail another 180 miles (289.67km) as I had always wanted to visit Greenland. However, I knew that to be wishful thinking, because the coast opposite was only open for two to three weeks of each summer because of the fog and pack ice; and also gales were frequent and severe in the northern part of the Denmark Strait. It was certainly not possible in our tired condition.

Anna refused to walk through the town wearing trousers, so she changed in a restaurant overlooking the harbour. She had little sailing experience, and that in keel boats. We set off across the harbour deep-reefed in a Force 6. There was a tremendous crack about 100yd (91.44m) out, and we almost capsized to windward – the main sheet block had disintegrated. I had to sail back with a single rope to the boom end, with no extra purchase. It was heavy work. Some cameramen had arrived and wanted to return after the radio interview. We retired to a café for food. I was tempted to try sheep's heads displayed on the counter but lacked sufficient courage, so they and I stared at each other across the counter while I ate fish.

During the interview we were told that a Dane regularly used to sail from the Faeroes to Iceland, in an 18ft (5.49m) boat with a little cabin. I said that the Vikings used to sail the North Atlantic too in open boats and we used much the same methods of navigation as they, and the interviewer replied: 'The Vikings were bloody bastards and we say in Iceland that they navigated this area on their stupidity.' I burst out laughing at the inference, and it was included in the tape. The newsreel people were waiting at the harbour, so Russell and I went out to sail. The reporters seemed determined to believe that Anna had sailed across with us – shades of the Sunday newspapers! We planed out of the harbour at 8 knots, the cameramen standing by the lighthouse. Russell would rather have been ashore, but I was thoroughly enjoying this exhilarating sail. What a pity Russell had not taken his full three weeks' leave, as I would have loved to have had a few more days to explore the area, and sail across the bay to Akranes.

Wanderer was booked to go home as deck cargo. I saw the Icelandic Steamship dock foreman and explained it would be easier to load my dinghy direct from the water on to the ship.

'Ni,' he said. 'You bring it here.'

'Could I borrow a trolley to load my dinghy on to?'

'Ni.'

'I can leave my boat on the quay for you to collect if I can borrow three men to pull it out.'

'Ni.'

'It will only take a few minutes.'

'Ni! We do not load from the quayside – only from the yard.'

'I can bring my boat here with a little help.'

'Ni! You bring boat here, I not send men out of yard.'

'I can't bring the boat here unless your men help me, it is too heavy to lift.'

'Ni. You must bring it here before 6.30.'

'I can't get it here by 6.30 without help.'

'You must bring it tomorrow.'

'Tomorrow I am flying to Scotland.'

'It will not go on to Trollafos unless you bring it here.'

'Please let me have some help.'

'Ni.'

'This is a bad way to treat visitors. The Icelandic Tourist Office said everybody was very friendly. Can I borrow your trolley?'

'Ni.'

The foreman walked away and so did I, blazing angry. A charge-hand came up and apologised for the foreman's rudeness. Russell and I got *Wanderer* 2ft up the slip, but only after a struggle. A local garage-owner said he could let us have a breakdown truck at 1900 hours but as the yard closed at 1830 hours this would not help us. Just as we got the boat on to the first roller, we were surrounded by dockers with a trolley. In two minutes *Wanderer* was loaded and mobile. I asked the beaming chargehand how he had persuaded the foreman to change his mind, and he admitted going to another shipping company to borrow their men and their electric trolley. 'I not tell the foreman,' he said! Well out of sight of the foreman I presented him with our Burgee. He was delighted. It was in good hands.

On the Wednesday we walked to the airport about 2 miles (3.22km) away. I told Russell to choose our seats, as he was the expert on aeroplanes. We walked through the main cabin, through the small cabin and the kitchen, past the toilets and sat down in the tail. 'Why here?' I asked Russell. 'When we crash, it is the safest place to be,' he replied.

The flight to Glasgow was faster and warmer than our sea passage out. A joint recorded interview for BBC Scottish television took place when we landed.

'Did you let anybody know you were attempting to sail a dinghy to Iceland?'

'Yes, we told the Wick coastguards.'

'Did they make any comments?'

'Yes. '

'Can you tell me what they said?'

'Not on television I can't.'

The cruise had been an interesting one, on reflection. Despite the very bad conditions of head winds and gales, it confirmed my opinion that a small open boat can be cruised at sea, providing the crew was experienced. Russell had fully justified my choice of crew, being capable, very tough and the possessor of a sense of humour. The Wayfarer, as expected, proved herself a tough able seaworthy dinghy, but ten days at sea is the maximum duration in heavy weather for pleasure cruising – after that it becomes hard work.

PART III

INTERLUDE

7

Winter Plans

Wanderer has sailed round most of the North Sea and across the northern part of it several times with little trouble and no real danger; and this in a shallow stormy area generally considered unsuitable for cruising. We have ridden out Force 8 gales, one off Heligoland and another off the Norwegian coast, and suffered really bad weather en route to Iceland, with very little water coming aboard. The Wayfarer is a superb sea boat.

Much of the credit for the success so far must belong to the fact that we train in that wonderful area of the Wash and north Norfolk coast, which can produce almost any condition with very little warning. In addition, I have always been extremely careful never to be caught close to a lee shore in bad weather, and I rarely take any unnecessary risks.

Having cruised thus far, I still feel no wish to go south; the northern areas fascinate me – the Shetlands, Fair Isle, the Faeroes and northern Norway. I like to see what is round the next headland, a curiosity that may yet lead me into trouble.

The Wayfarer remains the best cruising dinghy there is. When John Buckingham and I started cruising we were both convinced a buoyant open boat, a good sea boat like the Wayfarer, was capable of cruising safely across open water. The principles of open water cruising are exactly the same as they have always been throughout the history of sailing – in bad weather always make sure that you have plenty of sea room and never get caught on a lee shore. There is obviously a limit to the amount of strong winds and therefore bad sea conditions that a boat can survive, and when this point is reached in an open boat it becomes necessary to lay to a sea anchor and lower the mast so that the boat weathercocks rather than shears round her sea anchor, until the weather moderates. I still maintain that open water cruising is as safe as most other sports, and far more rewarding.

I grew up in awe of the sea which has never left me. It can be kind, tolerant, beautiful even generous, frightening, majestic and terrifying. The sea has no favourites. It is totally uncaring. It should never ever be taken lightly. It reminds me of the courtier who, after each audience with the Great and Powerful Majesty, frequently checked that his head was still on his shoulders.

I admit to a fear of the sea, and at times I have been badly scared. I have also made mistakes. I remember once hiring a Broads half-decker with the typical long boom to take Liv, a Norwegian girl who was trying to teach me enough Norwegian to understand the Norse weather forecasts, for a sail on the Broads. Coming back to the staithe, I forgot I was sailing a half-decker instead of a dinghy and sailed too close to a houseboat, so that our boom rattled against all his windows. Luffing up into the wind, we got clear but unfortunately the main sheet had hooked over his stern rail and we came to a crashing halt, drifting back to rattle all his windows for a second time. I apologised and the owner was charming when he saw that no damage had been done. It was disturbing to realise, however, that I had made such an elementary mistake.

On another occasion, on my introductory sail with my new crew Bill, we sailed from Brancaster at dusk intending to cross the Wash to Skegness. It was a dark night with poor visibility at dawn. I woke Bill to show him Skegness beach and town just appearing through the early morning mist. It turned out to be Mablethorpe some 15 miles (24.14km) further north!

I began to wonder if I was as capable of crossing the North Sea as I liked to think. But as soon as I have recovered my nerve from the last trip, which takes about three months, my feet itch to be in a boat again and I begin planning the next, and always into the colder latitudes. The following could be three interesting cruises:

1 To Rockall. This is a small rock some 300 miles (482.79km) out into the Atlantic. It is the very tip of the highest mountain of an underwater mountain range and stands just 65ft (19.81m) above the water. Navigation would have to be extremely accurate if one

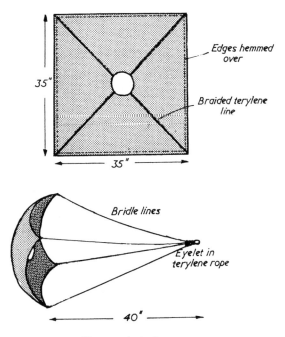

The parachute drogue.

was to find this small spot in the North Atlantic; celestial navigation would be essential, for we should be well beyond the range of the radio beacons, and DR could not be relied on. Such a trip would entail skill, endurance and determination, and failure would be no disgrace.

2   From the Outer Hebrides to St Kilda, and then back along the north coast of Scotland to the Pentland Firth. St Kilda is some 40 miles (64.37km) out into the Atlantic, and is now uninhabited except for a small army detachment and visiting work parties from the National Trust. From what has been published, this island would be well worth a visit.

3   From Wick across the Pentland Firth to Fair Isle, the Shetlands and the Faeroes. These would be fascinating islands and a lovely cruising ground. But these are challenging conditions; the Pentland Firth is the most dangerous stretch of water in the world and the *North Sea Pilot* waxes almost lyrical about its hazards; much of the North Sea empties and fills every 12 hours through

the gaps between the Orkneys, Fair Isle and Shetland, making it a rough piece of water. It was beyond my capability at the moment.

I was still determined to visit Arctic Norway. I looked at it carefully, but it is a long passage from eastern Scotland diagonally across the northern North Sea and Norwegian Sea to Trondheim – too far!

So it was to be the Faeroes I decided. I sat down with pencil and paper to plan. It would be a 4–5 day passage from NW Scotland, we could call at North Rona if the weather was good, and explore the Faeroe Islands when we arrived. Suddenly I realised that a base in the Faeroe Islands brought Northern Norway within our range! It was the same distance as our cruise last year to Iceland – so all our planning of stores and equipment applied. It also had the advantage of better weather than the North Atlantic route to Iceland.

The dinghy, as usual, was trailed home to Watton from Brancaster Staithe, where it normally sails on Sundays. *Wanderer* was washed down, rubbed down, repainted and revarnished. The centreboard pivot bolt was inspected, as was the rudder bolt, and all the standing rigging was checked. The $5/16$in-diameter hollow copper rivet through the hound plate had pulled down, as had the wooden screws, so a solid rivet was fitted and the rear wood screws in the plate were replaced by $3/16$in-diameter copper rivets (tube). This was obviously now a much stronger job on the mast. I had tried previously to rivet up with bronze rod, but this alloy had proved too hard – apparently copper is the only satisfactory material.

The standing rigging is of stainless steel, and there was no sign of chafe. The halliards had been replaced some time before with pre-stretched terylene, and they were still in excellent condition, despite a hard winter's use. The mast is wooden, and I shall never use a metal one, for emergency repairs can not easily be carried out at sea.

The flag halliard was a little chafed, and was replaced. The rudder was drilled and fitted with a locking bolt to keep the blade down and also to strengthen the rudder cheeks. Some damage had been caused by the previous winter's frost, but only the surface varnish was cracked and this did not appear serious.

The sails were overhauled by Jeckells, who did a good job on them. The seams, which rub against the shrouds and the batten pockets, required restitching. A spare main sheet and spare jib, and also a spare main sheet block, were taken.

The amount of water and food to be carried caused me some serious thought because, although we had taken sufficient in the previous summer on our Iceland cruise, we had not eaten enough. Water is the most important commodity and, as before, we carried it in four separate containers tied down with shock-cord to the floorboards and close to the rear buoyancy bulkhead. This water should last us for two weeks, since it provided one pint per person daily. In addition to water, we would have liquid in the tinned soups and fruit. The water in this position keeps the weight aft, balancing the rucksacks of tinned food secured forward of the mast.

I worked out a specimen menu, doubled it, and multiplied it by ten. Soup was to be in liquid form for the crossing, with dried varieties for use in Norway, where water could be obtained more easily. We carried tinned fruit and as many fresh apples and oranges as we could cram into odd corners. Three dozen fresh eggs were greased, stored in plastic egg boxes and tied down with shock-cord beneath the side decks. Cheese and eggs would provide the staple cold meal and bad weather diet.

Keeping charts dry in an open dinghy is always a problem. The Ford Motor Company had sent us some stiff plastic envelopes with clear plastic on one side, and I proposed to fold the charts into these and in bad weather chalk on the plastic with a chinagraph pencil. Dividers, pencils, rubbers, and wind speed indicator were clipped in a plastic box beneath the side deck. The big parallel rulers were clipped beneath the foredeck.

The Homer/Heron DF radio remained clipped under the foredeck. On earlier trips this had been stored in the stern locker – an inconvenient place. In its new position the crew could pull down the headphones and listen to weather forecasts without moving from his normal sleeping position.

I had recently ordered two waterproof ¼W lifejacket lights, which should give us just sufficient light for chart work or repairs at night. If we had to lay to a drogue, I intended to hang these lights beneath the cover on the mast. They should be a great improvement on the bulky, inconveniently shaped hurricane lantern we had carried previously – and there would be no paraffin to carry. These new lights should not be bright enough to destroy our night vision, besides being small and handy. White hand flares, as always, would be carried to warn off shipping, but since I estimated there would be only three hours of darkness in these latitudes, they should merely be regarded as extra safeguards. I detest crossing shipping lanes having twice been almost run down near the Texel Lightship. This is another reason for going north – there is less shipping!

After a year ashore one forgets how intensely cold it can be in an open boat with no possibility of going below into a cabin for sleep, warmth and dryness. I intended to wear pyjamas, long woollen pants and vest, quilted underclothes, flannel shirt, corduroy trousers, with three large jerseys, two pairs of football socks, a neck towel and balaclava hat, with a tracksuit for cold nights as well. My crews always raised their eyebrows when I listed my sailing wardrobe.

Choice of crew was unusual – previously I had picked my crew from past knowledge of them but this time was completely different – my crew picked me! A stranger walked up to me on the Wayfarer stand at the London Boat Show, looked me straight in the eye and said 'I'm Bill Brockbank. I race a Firefly very successfully, a Fireball reasonably well, and I'm your new crew.' I replied 'Oh no you are not!' and we argued about it for a short while and then he went away. I had never met Bill Brockbank before but during the following months I kept bumping into him unexpectedly and the conversation kept repeating. Eventually I weakened and justified my decision with the thought 'At least he has plenty of determination – even if I don't know anything else about him.'

It was a decision I never had cause to regret for he turned out to be an excellent dinghy sailor, resourceful, likeable, with an enormous reserve of good humour, which seasickness did nothing to dampen, and very tough.

PART IV

NORWAY

8

Preparations

Before finally committing ourselves to crossing the Norwegian Sea again, I enquired of the local meteorological office about the frequency of gales, and prevailing winds. I was given the following information:

Faeroes–Lofoten, July
Surface wind W–SW light to moderate Faeroes area: becoming S–SW light winds Lofoten area but may be affected by strong coastal winds near Norway
Average Air and Sea Temperatures +11°C
Fog Probability 10–20 per cent
Current South-westerly
Gales Rare

The results of my enquiries were much as I had expected from my reading of the *Pilots*, and were also confirmed by further enquiries at the Central Weather Office. As I had led Bill to expect at least two gales of Force 8, I thought it fair to let him know that the weather average was better than expected.

Listening to the 1340 shipping forecast one lunchtime just three days before we left for Scotland, I heard: 'Gale warnings are in force for the following areas: Fair Isle, Hebrides, Bailey and Faeroes – Force 9. Fair Isle possibly Force 10.' This was startling – an unequivocal Force 9 in an area that we had been regarding as a good weather area! I immediately telephoned the Norwich chandlers for 150ft (45.72m) of 1ton breaking strain nylon for a drogue warp, because I thought my 10cwt (500kg) terylene would not stand the strain much above Force 8. I was unable to obtain it at such short notice, but was not unduly worried, as it was merely an insurance against the unexpected.

Last-minute preparations for a cruise are usually hectic, quite apart from running a business which kept me in the office from 0630 daily until midnight for two weeks or so before departure so that I could ensure that everything was cleared before I left. Finally I put new bearings in the trailer wheels, strengthened the mast support, reset the suspension arms to increase ground clearance to cope with the roads in the Western Highlands, checked the tyres, had the engine of the automatic Cortina tuned and packed everything in the boot.

An executive of Shell, Arthur Barton-Jones, who had been a customer and friend for several years, telephoned to say that 'Shell required a new film of general interest for their film library and he thought my cruise to Faeroes and North Norway would be ideal. Would I take a 16mm cine camera and 4,000ft (1,300m) of colour film with me?' Neither Bill nor I had ever used a cine camera before so he delivered the camera and film stock next day personally, and gave me an intensive course on how to make a film, how to load and operate the camera, and dire warnings about the effect that only a few drops of salt water would have on the film gate or shutter. The dinghy had already been stowed against a check list so I had to re-pack the stern buoyancy compartment to accommodate the cine camera and 40 reels of film – but away from the compass. I also checked the standing and running rigging, replaced the gooseneck screws, packed the food and double wrapped the spare clothing in plastic bags. During the previous week *Wanderer* had spent one night in the garage paint shop and was looking immaculate.

Once again my father and brother Noel made a determined last-minute effort to prevent me sailing offshore. On this occasion they took a completely different line and it was some time before I realised their objective, which was to destroy my confidence in my boat and myself. Unfortunately I lack self-confidence, which they well know, and I am afraid they succeeded better than they realised.

At the last moment I had to delay departure to attend a meeting of East Anglian Ford Dealers to discuss the planned strike in the Post Office and how to minimise the effect this would have on our sophisticated businesses where speed of communication and cashflow were so important. I commented, somewhat bitterly, that it was doubtful if union members realised, or cared about, the damage they did to the country; that it was the same in vehicle manufacturing where we have always had unofficial strikes planned to coincide with new model announcements; it was no wonder that Britain was falling behind her competitors; and that national recovery would be impossible until union leaders were able to exercise some discipline and control over their members. It was not surprising that foreign customers and friends considered us to be unreliable.

It was a pleasure to see Norman Meekings and John Galloway, who as usual were acting as co-drivers, waiting outside the meeting. As before, we intended driving overnight in one hour shifts while the others slept, thus we should be able to cover the long haul northward at a steady speed of 65–70 mph. Outside Cambridge we pulled into the side as the trailer was snaking badly at speed. Restowing the dinghy by moving the heavier items forward did the trick, and after that the boat and trailer followed us docilely. Ten miles north of Newark we came upon a Ford Truck with a large pantechnicon body blatantly exceeding the speed limit (his max speed limit was the same as ours) and we passed him with a wave. He passed us when we stopped to refuel, and we caught up with him again just as he was stopped by the police for speeding. We swept past with the comment 'there but for the grace of God go we!'

Bill was hitch-hiking across country from Liverpool to meet us at the main police station in Wetherby but we found him in the local fish and chip shop instead. We remarked that the dinghy looked half empty and quickly checked through to make sure I had not left anything at home and Bill seemed satisfied. On this trip we had to think of our film for Shell, so I had planned therefore to travel up through the Highlands, stopping overnight at Muir of Ord near Inverness and arriving at Kinlochbervie the following afternoon. This would give us some fine shots of the countryside on this route and I hoped to turn our film into a first-class travelogue and merely taking sea shots would not provide Shell with a general interest film. I was beginning to realise how much extra planning and work was involved in film making and was wondering how we would cope with a heavy 16mm camera when the dinghy was jumping in a big sea, and possibly being seasick as well.

We drove through the night, and arrived at the hotel in the Pass of Glencoe in time to wash and shave before they served breakfast. Since I had 10 minutes to kill before eating, I started to think about our trip, which was a great mistake; one should view these things cold-bloodedly. I had a good boat, extremely well equipped, a first-class crew in Bill, a young university student who seemed to have a touching faith in my judgements, and a carefully planned cruise with little left to chance. However, it was the most ambitious trip so far, and I was beginning to worry. Norman, John and Bill did their best to cheer me up.

Five miles along the north side of Loch Leven real disaster struck. A smoking trailer tyre caused us to stop for inspection, and found that the nearside suspension unit had broken, owing to corrosion. I had designed and built this some six years before as a special high-speed low-loading trailer, but launching *Wanderer* into salt water every Sunday since had corroded the suspension mounting flange. We unloaded the dinghy and found a branch in a nearby fence which, lashed to the trailer, acted as a jury rig and made an excellent springing unit. The Aluminium Company at Kinlochleven was able to make more permanent repairs later that day by welding. To keep the morale of the crew high during the delay, I suggested to Bill that we needed a small plastic pail – comfortable to sit on. He returned from the shops with the comment: 'The lady said she hadn't a small bucket, but could we manage with a wee potty!' We both sat on it and approved the design.

9

Summer Cruise

Force 7! The wind of the last two days had not decreased. I was not sorry to delay our departure for a number of reasons: I had 'cold feet', my father and brother Noel had badly dented my confidence, the Hotel Garbet at Kinlochbervie was warm and comfortable, and Mr and Mrs Sewell, the managers, were especially kind. The local fishermen were also most helpful and friendly.

The midday forecast spoke of winds of Force 5 to 6 with a trough passing over; and so, with no likelihood of gales in the immediate future, we trailed *Wanderer* to the harbour and began rigging. Stowing the gear took time. In the stern locker we packed sleeping bags, charts, sextant, navigation books, cine camera and film, gloves, spare oilskins, and first-aid kit. Spare clothing, Norwegian charts, spare stove, salt-water still, emergency rations (of six Horlick's dehydrated meals), Norwegian coast Pilot books, and one bottle each of whisky and brandy (for presents) went into the forward compartments. The Norwegians greatly appreciate English whisky. I am virtually a non-drinker, and at sea I think the habit of drinking spirits is best not acquired.

The rest of our stores, which went into the cockpit, comprised the following: three haversacks of food (one of self-heating tins of soup, one of cold tinned foods and one of soup and meat stews), a 5lb (2.27kg) CQR anchor, a grapnel anchor, 150ft (45.72m) of spare 10cwt (508.02kg) breaking strain terylene line, 3 dozen fresh eggs, 4 gallons of fresh water, a home-made stainless-steel stove, a rubber dinghy (for filming), sail-repair kit, oilskin-repair kit, spare pulleys, blocks, torches, navigational gear, washing-up kit, Teepol, Very pistol and red cartridges, white flares, two buckets, insulated mugs, Homer/Heron radio, spare line, chart case, repair kit (of files, drills, coping saw and screws and shackles), lifejackets, lifelines, headcover, airbeds, mast crutch, 2 quarts of petrol in screw-top glass bottles, 2 dozen oranges, 3 dozen apples, cheese, dates, raisins, nuts, and three tins of Horlick's lifeboat biscuits. We also took two gallons of oil and an oil bag, with the idea of dripping it out on to the waves to flatten them, should the weather become really bad. I had read about the use of oil but later, putting it into practice, I realised that far greater quantities of oil would be needed to achieve the desired effect.

I telephoned the Wick coastguards and gave them details of our trip. On Wednesday at 1630 as the wind dropped, I said my thanks to my good friends, John and Norman, wished them a good journey home, and filmed our departure from Scotland. We then headed for the Minch, setting our course 330° magnetic for Rona, as we cleared the last headland. At 2100 we got out the cold chicken provided by the Hotel Garbet and ate a drumstick each. I thoroughly enjoyed mine and then turned in, but Bill was immediately sick and returned his chicken to the sea.

On Thursday at 2400 hours it was blowing 4–5. We were broad reaching fast, despite two batten pockets rolled in the main, and occasionally the bow scooped aboard solid water. It was a pitch black night and we found the illuminated (Beta light) compass a great help.

Heading out into the Minch at 2300 hours on the first evening – always an anxious and exhilarating moment.

During the night I heard Bill being sick several times, poor devil! But I expected him soon to find his sea legs. I slept well, knowing us to be safely offshore. At 0200 I heated a tin of malted milk so that Bill could digest it while lying flat. He was immediately sick again. What a waste!

At dawn a quick mental plot at our estimated speed put us 10–15 miles (16.09–24.14km) from Rona. When getting out the Homer/Heron set to do a radio fix, we realised that, in discarding our heavy *Reeds Almanac*, we had left behind our only copy of the Morse code. I swore steadily to relieve my feelings, and made a mental note not to amend equipment at the last moment. Bill made out as much of the Morse code as he could remember – it would have to do! The resultant plot gave us Rona on a bearing of 320°, distance about 12 miles (19.31km). I could not get a sound off Cape Wrath, but got a bearing on Butt of Lewis and Sule Skerry.

On Friday at 0820 hours Bill saw land, but it turned out to be a cloud; then the thick mist closed in again. Ten minutes later the mist thinned and there was solid land – on the correct bearing, too. We each ate an orange and Bill was sick again.

Slowly we closed the land, for the wind had fallen light. Suddenly I realised that we were heading for Sula-Sgeir, not Rona. The tides must have set us at least 10 miles (16.09km) to westward of Rona, and it was essential that we landed there for Bill to eat a hot meal ashore, and keep it down in order to get some strength from it.

Solan geese were everywhere, wheeling above us and swooping along the rock faces, and rapidly despoiling my new sails, as we sailed along the island to film the vertical cliffs streaked with white lines of thousands of gulls on every ledge. At its eastern end the island curved round to form a large bay. The fishermen from Lewis used to land once a year to harvest the young solan geese, and they probably used this place to land.

Sula-Sgeir is called an island, but is little more than a large rock, ½ mile (800.05m) long and about 200yd (182.88m) wide. There is no soil, and the North Atlantic constantly batters it, and thousands of birds, especially guillemots, Leach's petrels, kittiwakes and fulmars visit it for breeding and migratory purposes. I was very tempted to go ashore here, but decided to press on to Rona, where we knew there was a landing.

Sula-Sgeir, 45 miles (72.41km) NW of Cape Wrath, a barren rock white with gannets and droppings. Visited once a year by the men of Lewis to take gugas for salting (young gannets and very much an acquired taste).

By 1230 on a broad reach we were closing Rona, clearly visible some 11 miles (17.7km) away, due east. At 4 miles (6.44km) distance it disappeared back into the mist. By Bill's watch, we were close enough to see a big swell running in from the south west and breaking heavily, with spray jumping to 25ft (7.62m). We passed the south shore and saw cliffs rising 300ft (91.44m), with one cleft running deep into the island. This must have been the south landing, but it looked impossible, only 20yd (18.29m) wide and 50yd (45.72m) deep, with 200ft (60.96m) cliffs and the swells crashing in. We drifted round the south-east corner of Rona and were sheltered from the swell. We could see seals, gannets, puffins, shags and much other wild life. A steady moaning from the seals, echoing back from the cliffs, sounded just like human voices.

Then we spotted Langa Beirigh, the cove mentioned in the *Pilot*. How small it looked – only 20yd (18.29m) wide and 50yd (45.72m) long, and finishing in a cavern running under the island. There were giant natural steps in the rock, and I clambered up the south side with a mooring rope tied round my waist while Bill fended off the boat. After tying the line round a rocky projection, and then a stern line round a boulder at sea level, we ferried our food and cooking gear ashore.

I had read about Rona. It is a northerly, isolated and exposed island that regularly supported a population from the eighth century AD. Its name, derived from 'Rony', means Seal Island, and it has no proper beach or shore, although hidden reefs and skerries surround it.

Possibly the first callers were Vikings, who might have used the island as a navigation mark in their raids of the north and west coasts of Scotland. Even today, landing on Rona is not easy and anchoring there virtually impossible, because the island is situated on a bed of hard rock. In earlier times the island was cultivated, supporting sheep, cows, a bull for breeding; and capable of yielding corn, barley meal, potatoes, mutton, seabirds and their eggs, and fish, and sealskins. The only essential that the island did not yield was peat for fuel. About 1680 the little community of about five families and thirty or so people met tragedy when a swarm of rats landed from a wreck and devoured all the island's stores. The starving island people were raided a few months later by passing seamen, who took their only bull, and they did not survive the double disaster and starved. The stone bothies, and cell and chapel have all lain in ruins since then.

The southern part of North Rona is a rounded hill, grass-covered, rising to 300ft (91.44m) while the rest is low lying, about 50ft (15.24m) above sea level. We were on the neck of the island, which was only 100yd (91.44m) from coast to coast. A flock of about fifty sheep spotted us and scampered up the ridge and over the crest. We found several ruins without roofs. Bill crawled into one while I filmed, but shrieks and screams broke the island quiet, and Bill rapidly retreated. There had been three fulmars inside the ruin. They had disliked the intrusion and had spat at him. Luckily we were up wind, because these birds spit out a vile smelling stream of fish-oil from their crops that quickly deteriorates into the remains of yesterday's food.

These ruined huts had a living room about 14ft (4.27m) diameter, the dry stone walls still about 7ft (2.13m) high, each stone closely fitting and sloping slightly outwards to shed water. There was also a wind baffle outside the doorway.

Walking across Fianuis, the rocky northern peninsula of the island, we traced the line of an old wall, probably an old sheepfold. Seagulls were nesting everywhere, completely unafraid of man, and if we stopped, they immediately 'froze' and pretended to be a stone.

A really substantial meal set us both up. We had soup, six-egg omelets, chicken, tomatoes, bread and butter, and fruit. As it was the first food Bill had enjoyed, I filmed him enjoying himself. The anchor line had chafed and both lines needed adjusting to keep the dinghy in the centre of the cove. Feeling very insignificant compared to nature, we decided to walk to the ruined church, as I needed the exercise and Bill required time to digest his meal before we sailed. A slight mist came up as we gazed in awe down into the gloom of Geodha Leis – a vertical fall into a narrow cleft down to the sea 200ft (60.96m) below. Seabirds were everywhere, and especially fascinating were the shags in their natural playground, ungainly on land but beautiful and powerful when submerged. Occasionally a seal swam into the cavern and chased the shags ashore in good-natured fun. Offshore hundreds of seals eyed us in curiosity.

Climbing the steep ridge, we gained the plateau, which we could not see across because of the mist. We passed several ruins almost overgrown. The last people left this island almost a century ago. Still looking for the ruined church, we suddenly realised how quickly the mist had thickened. We were lost. Reversing our course, we then bore off to starboard to find the coast to follow it back to the boat. In thick fog and completely lost, and worried about the dinghy, I swore at myself for not bringing a compass ashore. With the tide rising, the dinghy would be rubbing on the rocks and could easily be holed. It was eerie, everything magnified by the fog, the sea thundering on the rocks below and the seals moaning all around us. We could be here a long time living off sheep and seagulls (if we could catch either) I reflected. Following the coast-line and crossing two steep hills and old cultivations we eventually reached the cove.

Wanderer was only just beginning to chafe, as the tide edged her on to the rocks. At 2100 hours we paddled offshore in dense sea fog and, while Bill turned in, I set the compass course to clear the north end of Rona. What a fascinating place, one worthy of a longer stay! The midnight forecast was SSW, Force 2–3. Our course for Faeroes was due north, just 130 miles (209.21km) away.

It was Saturday and the wind continued southerly, Force 1–2, and we only just had steerage way. I was so tired I fell asleep on watch. By noon the sea was glassy and there was a flat calm, with Rona still visible to the south. Most of the next off-watch I spent filming. The 1340 forecast was 'Hebrides & Minch northerly 3–5; Faeroes (the adjacent area to the north) southerly 3–4'. 'Work that one out,' Bill commented without malice.

Twelve hours later we were still barely making headway, and were both very cold and tired. It was important to stick to our 2-hour watch system. By 0800 hours the following day Bill had reefed twice and the wind was northerly Force 5; we repeated the procedure to get it on film. Repeating operations in order to get the right sequence on the Shell film was all additional work. I was becoming very worried about Bill, whose continued seasickness must soon result in him losing his strength. Could we safely continue our cruise from Faeroes to Norway?

We were both cold and shivering, and it was an effort to remove our clothes, which were sodden with condensation. Wearing oilskins all the time meant that top layers of clothing became clammy with condensation, while the bottom ones next to the skin soaked up body

The cold weather and seasickness was taking its toll on Bill.

perspiration. Not a comfortable mixture. With winds backing, we were heading north west, and I reflected that we were probably on the same route as that to Iceland last year. I cursed the weather. At midnight I reloaded the camera and listened to the news. The BBC announcer chatted while awaiting the forecast time, telling us it had been a beautiful day – the perfect day for camping – and suggesting that more people should sleep out in such weather. Loudly we both disagreed with him – we were freezing. He also reminded us that today was the anniversary of Marconi's death. I approved of Marconi's invention of radio and thought how pleasant it was to have a radio link to civilisation and how useful to be able to receive weather forecasts when miles out at sea.

On Monday at 0300 Bill told me that he had averaged 3 knots during his watch, and that the 0200 forecast was south-west winds, Force 4–5, increasing to 6–7. Our wind was northerly 1–2. I saw a light during my watch, but put it down to imagination, as the Faeroes would be beyond the horizon. I sailed steadily at 4 knots – *W48* must have sniffed the land!

At 1000 hours I saw land at last. The wind was 3–4, so I planed towards it with all despatch. The landfall is a supreme moment of any cruise. It is impossible to describe the thrill and satisfaction that it gives one. Gradually the whole island of Sydero became clear, Akaberg gave a radio bearing of 60° and a cross-bearing on Sule Skerry put us 35 miles (54.33km) offshore.

At 1115 the land disappeared into the clouds. I considered blowing up the inflatable dinghy in order to film *Wanderer*, as the sea was flat calm.

Land appeared again, this time the whole island of Sydero. I estimated that we should land in the Faeroes between 2200 and 2300 hours, so we would still be within our estimate of 4–5 days for the voyage.

The land ahead was high, rugged and most impressive, a range of mountains capped by clouds, which looked like a glacier pouring ice down the valleys. This is the most impressive landfall I have ever seen. It seemed a long time since Bill and I were discussing this moment three weeks ago and 1,000 miles (1,609.3km) south. I shall never forget this moment.

We just had steerage. Bill beat up five eggs in butter and heated them in the mess tin. After an age the eggs had still not thickened, so he handed over the mess to me in disgust and turned in. What a godsend our stove was! Hot food was essential. My six layers of clothing beneath my oilskins were cold and sodden, owing to perspiration and condensation; when the two layers of wetness met, one just shivered non stop. There is no ventilation in one-piece oilskins. A big swell began to roll in from the north east, although we were wallowing in a flat calm. It must have been due to recent gales beyond the horizon.

When Bill came up from being off watch, he was very cold and decided to strip and towel down. We took a cine film of the whole sequence, thinking of Shell's faces when they saw it – a seagoing

Changing clothes. We carried two sets. Each lasted about four days. The inner layers soak up body perspiration and the outer layers absorb condensation on the inside of the oilskins.

Dance of the Seven Veils. A trawler crossed our bows, but we did not hail it as we knew our position – 12–15 miles (19.31–24.14km) from Sydero.

It was now Tuesday morning and we decided to make for Sumbǒ, the village on the south west of the island. It is sheltered and just clear of the tide race. Clearly visible now were the white houses against the dark hills. Suddenly with a roar a helicopter dived on to us and did two quick circuits before returning to land. Checking, I suppose, to see if we were fishing within the 12-mile (19.31-km) limit. Bill turned in. The wind slowly increased from WSW, and I used the jib stick for the first time. A fishing boat bore down on us. I woke Bill and told him to expect visitors.

A long narrow light boat, built on Viking lines, came alongside as I hoisted our red ensign, and the four men in the boat asked us where we had come from. When we said 'From Scotland' they gave a cheer and said 'Well done', and offered us a tow into their harbour. Taking our 10cwt (508.02kg) anchor warp, they towed us in at 9 knots. The crew must have had remarkable strength in their hands, because I saw them taking the surge with bare hands. Another fishing boat joined them and the crew, friendly and cheerful, seemed surprised to learn that we had crossed the North-East Atlantic in such a small boat. I transferred into their boat so that I could film, and 40 minutes later we were in Sumbǒ Harbour. Mr Thomson, the owner of the boat that had towed us in, commented to the onlookers: 'I went out fishing this morning for cod and look what I caught.'

The crews of each boat began to gut their catch. I timed them as I filmed – 7 seconds for each fish. Mr Thomson and son Andrew beckoned us to follow them. We walked through the village with them. I asked if there was a restaurant, but they looked blank, so I asked if there was a café. They immediately grinned and said 'Ja', and set off at an enormous pace to their home. I suddenly realised that 'café' in the Faeroes means 'coffee'. Damn it! They would think I was scrounging. They cooked us soup and bacon and eggs, followed by cheese and coffee – an excellent meal and such a change from our own cooking. We told them about our friends Karton Jespersen and his family in Trandisvaag, and we were offered a tow there after supper. 'Only two hours,' they said.

Mr Thomson told us that there was a bad *stoma* (tide race) off Akreberg, but that we would be towed through the inside passage. On the way *Wanderer* was planing comfortably, hard on the back of the second wave of the fishing boat's wash, and I began to film, until I suddenly saw rocks in the viewfinder only 8ft (3m) away. Our passage was through calm water, but we were disconcerted to see the stroma pounding over islets in sheets of froth and foam. We crept close beneath the headland, the cliffs only 20yd (18.29m) away, and rising sheer to 1,000ft (304.8m). A fantastic sight!

At midnight *Wanderer* was pulled alongside our host boat, and we were offered chicken and aquavit. Declining, we passed over our bottle of Scottish whisky, which came back much depleted, and our speed increased. The scenery was wonderful. The whole northern sky was bathed in a soft orange glow, which silhouetted the offshore islands. Sydero rose away purple to port, and house lights twinkled as we passed by each fjord. On demand our whisky bottle again exchanged boats, and again our speed increased!

10

The Faeroes

At 01.30 hours the fishing boat cut her engines as we approached the lights of Trandisvaag. Somebody came out of the darkness and tied our boat up; it was Mr Jespersen, whom Mr Thomson had telephoned to say that we were arriving. *Wanderer* was tied to a spring across the harbour, and we were taken home by Karton Jespersen, whose wife had cooked us bacon cakes. Karton, who was a petrol-tanker driver, decided to take his first two days' holiday ever, to look after us. We were very touched, and spent the time thoroughly enjoying ourselves, resting and eating, and meeting all the Jespersen family, Mr and Mrs Jacobson, the postmaster, and Maud Olsen, hailed to join us because she spoke excellent English. Having unloaded a boat full of wet clothes, visited the harbour-master, seen that the Wick Coastguards had been informed of our safe arrival on the Faeroe Islands, and made various necessary phone calls, we looked forward to a tour of the island. (One meets island people very naturally from a small boat, and we were immediately made welcome everywhere by complete strangers.)

We all squeezed into Karton's car and, with Maud acting as inter-preter, set off to see the island. Climbing steadily up the side of the valley, we passed the only plantation on the Faeroes, where Scots pines grew only about 4ft (1.22m) high. The route took us through a tunnel cut only 12 months before. The single track, with frequent passing places, was 4,921ft (1,500m) beneath the mountain. Previously the only means of reaching the next valley was by pony or boat.

Passing Kvalba, a pretty village in an attractive valley, we drove to the cliffs overlooking the Atlantic, which reared straight up out of the sea. God help any boat caught on such a lee shore in gale conditions! Further along we saw a landing for fishing boats. What a landing! Boats had to be hauled up steel girders at an angle of 45°, and the boat sheds were halfway up the mountain.

Back at the Jespersens' an excellent meal had been prepared by Johanna Marie. Over it Bill remarked that, being in a Norse country, he was surprised that he had seen no blue-eyed people. We were told by Karton that their ancestors were Spaniards, so everybody had dark hair and brown eyes. The Faeroese enjoy every minute of the daylight hours and sit up late during the summer months. Despite our tiredness, the evening was most enjoyable. I was surprised to find out then that our hosts knew of my previous year's cruise to Iceland.

We woke the following morning to rain. It was grey and miserable. We were fed coffee and cakes for breakfast. Maud, who we discovered was a student of English and Danish, and at college in Denmark during term time, told us about the Torshaven Festival on the following Tuesday. I felt very tempted to stay on for it, and abandon more cruising, as she would be a charming companion, and the crossing to Norway could be testing, especially as I feared Bill's strength must weaken with continual seasickness. I bathed, and after a trip to bring out more wet clothes from our dinghy, we had a wonderful lunch of ox, and then took Maud and Karton for a sail. Squalls hit us as we crossed the fjord, and I thought it wise to return.

The following day was beautiful. This was said to be the worst summer since 1928 in the Faeroes, but we were not grumbling. Maud had borrowed a national costume and I wanted to film her wearing it. When we returned to our hosts, we found that Mrs Jespersen had washed all our clothes, darned Bill's jersey and fitted a new zip in my trousers. She showed us her knitting, and I filmed it. The jerseys she had knitted were beautiful both in colour and design; she gave Bill and me one each, and we were very proud of such beautiful garments.

We decided to sail during that afternoon. My decision was based on sympathy rather than common sense. Despite Bill's continual seasickness, I felt that he might recover, and we had been ashore too long; the land was beginning to pull. In addition I was not sure I had sufficient stamina or willpower to carry the cruise through. I suppose both Bill and I felt the need to prove ourselves to ourselves.

Johanna, Marie, and Maud went to the harbour to buy fish for us, and Karton and I collected other stores. While stowing the boat, organising new charts and laying off our course to Trondheim, 450 miles (724.18km) away, I saw the women returning with a whole halibut, some of which they would cut up for us to take. Just before we left the Jespersens presented us both with a beautiful enamel spoon and a set of cufflinks bearing the Faeroes national flag. I shall always treasure these gifts, and hope always to keep in contact with such friendly people.

Waving goodbye, I realised how sorry I was to go. Perhaps next year I could take Maud to the Torshaven Festival, and sail back via the Orkney and Shetland Islands. Just now we were heading for Norway, compass course due east magnetic. Bill estimated our crossing could take six days in perfect conditions, but from past experience I reckoned on eight to ten days. At 2200 I came on duty. It was fish for supper. Mrs Jespersen had cooked the whole halibut for us and wrapped each joint separately in foil, and put them in a large plastic bucket. I was amazed at such generosity, as I had expected two slices each. It was superb fish; we ate it in our fingers, and finished off with an orange apiece.

Bill was in excellent form, his sense of humour having reappeared. He would make an excellent companion now that Mrs Olsen's seasick pills were doing their job. I turned in, feeling happy. The midnight forecast gave us south-westerly, Force 5–6, becoming westerly. Bill approved, but I was not sure that we could safely sail on a broad reach in a Force 6, as I had the experience of our broach during the 1962 Norwegian crossing to think about. But the fish supper was good, and I turned in feeling happy now that Bill could eat again.

The following day I woke up very tired indeed and very cold. I was missing a night's sleep. The seas were building up with winds south west, Force 4–5, and *Wanderer* was over-canvased. We filmed the whole reefing sequence. By 1100 hours the seas were 14ft (4.27m) high and we heaved to for filming. Changing to a new reel of film under the foredeck was extremely difficult, and one spot of salt water on the film gate would ruin the remainder of the film. By loading under the foredeck, however, we managed to keep the camera dry. Bill came on duty and I asked him to pose for a seasickness slide. While posing, leaning over the side of the dinghy, he was violently sick, bringing up the soup he had drunk only two minutes before. All my worries were back again!

11

Only 400 Miles To Go

At 1500 hours I came on watch. Bill had been continually sick, but had done a steady 4 knots, allowing for the bailing that had to be done. The seas were heavy and the wind south west, Force 6. After sailing for 30 minutes, I decided that, with heavy breaking seas, it was too risky to continue. Heaving to under main only, I laid out the drogue and removed the rudder. This was difficult, because as soon as the tiller was removed, the rudder locked over hard, as the dinghy was drifting hard astern. *Wanderer* was sheering about with her mast up, but it was quite safe, and I thought it unnecessary to lower the mast in a Force 7. We shipped two heavy seas, and I pumped out. I filmed the seascape before turning in.

The 1758 forecast gave 'Viking, Faeroes, westerly, Force 6 perhaps 7'. We should be here all night. We could not sail in those conditions! I told Bill that he must eat or we would have to return to the Faeroes; he suggested the Shetlands if necessary. I did not want to call off the cruise, but there was a risk of my crew being useless after six days without food. I missed the midnight forecast by 10 minutes as I had overslept. The seas were still heavy, about 14ft (4.27m), and the wind had moved into the south west, setting up an unpleasant cross sea. I pumped out the dinghy and gave Bill a lifeboat biscuit.

On Saturday at 0100 I turned in. An hour later I looked round for shipping. This gale was a nuisance, for we should have been a third of the way to Stadt (Norway). I missed the 0650 forecast again through oversleeping, but this time by only 5 minutes, so I was improving! By noon the seas were actively unpleasant. *Wanderer* was sheering about badly, and after she had shipped two big seas while I was pumping out, I decided to lower the mast. I had not realised how weak my fingers were, and it needed pliers before I could undo the jib hanks. Filming Bill lowering the mast into the crutches caused my

Bill going forward to take in the small jib in preparation for a gale. It was already Force 6, gusting 7. He wore one-piece oilskins, essential for keeping out the wet on and off watch.

stomach to heave, but Bill was avoiding being sick somehow. He was still clutching about a third of the lifeboat biscuit I had given him last night. I decided not to tie down the storm cover, as I was hoping the gale would blow itself out; it was only Force 7 anyhow.

I had forgotten that, without standing shrouds, we had nowhere to attach our aerial and, with reception poor and waves slamming against the hull, we missed the next forecast. We pumped out cautiously, for there was a real danger of tearing oilskins on cleats. Torn oilskins at home were merely annoying, but up here it might well cause exposure. We also had to guard against pitching overboard as, with the mast down and no shrouds to hold on to, it was not easy to move about. It was much warmer below. One would not know that a gale was blowing from beneath the comfort of the canvas headcover, except for the waves thumping the hull every 30 seconds.

This was the first time that I had experienced a sunny gale. I had to get up, as the mast had jumped out of the crutch, severely bending a spreader. The motion of the boat was violent. I adjusted the sea-anchor warps to prevent chafing, and sat out in brilliant sunshine and a howling gale writing up the log. Turning in, I felt suddenly cold, tired and dispirited. For some reason I realised I was grey-headed and getting old.

The answer was probably to find a wife and settle down. What a place to become introspective – in the middle of the Norwegian sea!

At 1900 hours, and still blowing hard, I heated a large tin of stew. It was difficult to keep the stove alight, and I had to take the heat deflector off the burner to keep the temperature of the fuel tank up to normal. I have used a small optimus stove running on petrol in my stainless-steel gimballed stove for some years, and it has never let me down. As usual, a hot meal gave one fresh energy. Telling Bill to keep his head down to avoid losing his meal, I tied down the cockpit cover. It was difficult to do singlehanded, but I did it somehow, and it was much warmer beneath it. I also changed into two more sweaters and added another pair of corduroy trousers. The waves had increased to 18ft (5.49m) and there was no shipping about. I passed Bill a lifeboat biscuit but he was not enthusiastic, and I fancy he threw it overboard when I was not looking.

The next dawn, at 0400 on Sunday, was welcome. Winds were WSW, Force 5–6, and seas were heavy. Our clothing was wet through and smelt high. Bill could not face breakfast, until I suddenly remembered that Mrs Galloway, a Norfolk friend, had baked us a rich date and nut cake stowed in the rear buoyancy. I blessed her and got it out. It was rich and filling and Bill could keep it down. All through Sunday I hoped to start moving again, and marked our estimated position on the charts. The evening meal was again welcome, and with no shipping about I turned in at 1800 hours. A seagull kept parading up and down the cover along the length of the mast, and strong language was needed to persuade him to stop scratching about. I was getting irritable at the delay in sailing.

By 1900 hours the seas seemed better, and I removed the cockpit cover. What a struggle it was! Bill helped me put up the mast and we hoisted the genoa, having decided that even a deep reefed main was too large to be safe in that sea. By 2000 hours we were under way, doing 4 knots and surging up to 7 knots on the front faces of the waves. At 2300 hours I took over. We were heading due east very fast. It was too dark to see the genoa to steer by, and I had to steer by listening for the sail flogging.

An hour later we were swept by a breaking crest, and *Wanderer* filled and lay waterlogged. Several times she tried to get up into a plane when the water would have emptied through the self-bailers, but each time the water ran forward, until the bows ran under and more water poured in. I shouted for Bill over the increasing wind, and we changed down to the small jib. The forecast gave us south-westerly winds, Force 7, and, with the wind increasing, we again took down the mast, laid out the drogue and tied down the cockpit cover. I cleaned out the pump, and dropped the strainer overboard which could have been serious, as without it the pump becomes blocked more frequently. It was pure carelessness. I turned in exhausted.

At dawn on Monday, the following day, there was no shipping but seas were too heavy for us to sail. Bill refused food, but at midday I persuaded him to eat a slice of date loaf. We both needed dry clothes, but it was impossible to get them from the forward buoyancy until the weather moderated. I found a packet of dry socks in the stern locker and opened the plastic bag to find one pair of soft socks and the other of coarse Harris wool. There followed a long discussion with Bill as to the respective merits of putting coarse socks outside or inside the fine ones, but in practice they went inside, as they were much the smaller pair. It was wonderful to have one's feet feeling warm and dry again. I opened a bar of Horlick's rum fudge. Bill had a passion for this and he needed cheering up.

I kept wondering if we could sail, but knew it to be too risky. A radio fix on Akraberg and Muckle Flugga showed us that Stadt, Norway, was 200 miles (321.86km) away on a heading of 100° magnetic. A wave washed over the stern and soaked the charts. We certainly had had our share of poor weather on this leg. After filming some bad weather shots, I discovered that one could use the Heron/Homer set with the DF aerial by using the 'Nav' band, bringing the Heron aerial within a few inches of the set. It worked a treat. Bill used this method and got excellent reception for the midnight forecast, which gave Faeroes Force 8.

On the next day, Tuesday, at 0500 the seas were much better, winds south-westerly, Force 4. We were both reluctant to get started, so I cooked a five-egg omelet. By 0800, with small jib hoisted and main reefed to the second batten, we were making a steady 2 knots. Two hours later with winds south-westerly, Force 2–3, we changed to genoa, but before shaking out the reefs, I decided we must change our clothes. We needed the exercise as much as the warmth, but Bill looked dreadful – sick and shivering – and was not enthusiastic at all about changing in this sea.

I backed the jib to heave to, plucked up my courage and started stripping. Off came oilskins, boots, neck towel, three long pullovers, one short jersey, two pairs of trousers, quilted underclothes, long wool pants and vest, string vest, short pants and vest, two pairs of socks and woollen pyjamas. Grabbing a towel, I stood up in the wind and gave myself a quick polish all over until I positively glowed. Then I began to tear dry clothes out of their double plastic bags. Since my fingers were so weak, I had to use my teeth. When finally dressed and inside oilskins, I felt better. Bill then followed suit. Feeling happier making ground towards Norway, with the wind over our stern, we considered eating the remainder of Mrs Jespersen's fish for lunch, but since it was four days old, we reluctantly threw it overboard. We both felt better now that we were warm again, and optimistically thought the wind might set fair into the west, and give us a fast passage to Norway, for we had already had more than our fair share of bad weather.

12

Force Nine! What Will It Be Like?

The 1340 shipping forecast came over well. The wire aerial attached to the shrouds had made a big improvement. We turned in early and listened to the cricket scores. They were having fine weather in England, and we both wished that we could share some of it. The forecast started unpromisingly: 'Gale warnings are in operation in sea areas south-east Iceland, Faeroes, Fair Isle, Viking, Cromarty, Forties, Forth, Dogger, Fisher.' The general synopsis at 0600 GMT was as follows: 'A depression of centre pressure 975 about 100 miles [160.93 km] north of Lerwick is expected to move north-east up the Norwegian coast, but with a secondary low developing over the Skaggerak and moving east.'

Now came the shipping forecasts for the next 24 hours:

Viking and Forties Wind westerly, Force 7 to gale Force 8, veering north-west and moderating overnight, to Force 5 to 6. Showers, otherwise good visibility.
Fair Isle Wind north-west gale, Force 8, to severe gale, Force 9, moderating later in the day to Force 6. Rain at times, otherwise good visibility.
Faeroes Wind northerly, severe gale, Force 9, backing north-west. Force 5 by morning. Showers, otherwise good visibility.

We were very shaken. Force 9! I wondered what it would be like. Very bad indeed, I expected. I tried to break the news gently to Bill, but made a mess of it. He obviously thought the same as me: 'Shall we be alive to see the dawn?' Much to my surprise I discovered that I was not scared, even though the possibility of death was uppermost in my mind. My only regret was that I had caused Bill to risk his neck as well. In plotting our estimated position I tried to convince myself that we were in Forties, but already I knew that we were in Faeroes, and was reluctant to admit it, even to myself.

By 1430 the wind had increased very quickly. Dropping the main, we continued running under genoa only. We were almost on a dead run, and the seas were rapidly increasing. The wind began to veer to the north west, with gusts from Force 6 to 7. We had to hold on to the genoa as long as possible, but with heavy cresting seas, it became necessary to keep a careful watch on the seas coming up astern, for a slight error would see us over. I considered replacing the genoa with the small jib, but it did not seem worth the effort required. All that we could now do was to hold on to the course for as long as possible, and check preparations for a possible Force 9.

The forecaster seemed to have enjoyed telling us about it. We would have felt so much better if he had finished his report with 'Faeroes, Force 9, you poor devils!' or some such terms of sympathy. At least he had the grace not to add his usual 'and good sailing gentlemen' at the end of the forecast!

By 1530 the Force 7 was gusting up to Force 8 NNW, and the wind was still climbing. The whine in the shrouds became more and more shrill and insistent, until I felt it would never stop. Bill rigged the drogue, whilst I dropped the jib. We dropped the mast carefully, lowering it into the crutches in the lulls between the breaking seas.

After roping the mast into the crutches and tying the cover over the boat, I told Bill to get his head down before he was sick. He was going to need all his strength and stamina before the morning, if we were to survive.

A full blooded Force 8 was blowing by 1630, and I suggested to Bill that he might like to have a look. His answer was a decided 'No'. My view was very impressive – seas long, high and steep, with wave crests cascading down their fronts, and foam everywhere. I sat on the stern locker feeling awed but, surprisingly enough, enjoying such a thrilling sight. I considered filming it, but decided that there was too much spray about.

At 1730, under the comfort of the boat cover, I began to write up the log. By now a full Force 9 was shrieking outside. It was bitterly cold, and the wind cut into one's face like a knife; it was difficult to look to windward, and to breathe into it was almost as bad. Beneath

I went forward to bring in the jib and uncleat the forestay while Bill rigged the sea anchor. Forecast: Severe gale – Force 9.

screwed-up eyes I reckoned that the seas were at least 28ft (8.53m) high. Thinking of Maud who by then was at the Torshaven Festival and whom we had hoped to meet again in Norway, I commented to Bill: 'What rotten luck for the Torshaven Festival.'

Bill dozed, even though he must have been bitterly cold, while I carried on writing up my log. Outside, the drogue warp was creaking badly. What a great pity that the Norwich chandlers had been unable to supply us with that 1-ton (1.02-tonne) nylon I had wanted. I was not sure that the 10cwt (508.02kg) terylene was adequate for the job, especially after the chafing it had suffered on Rona. Almost immediately *Wanderer* drove back against the sea-anchor. It must have parted, for I felt her swing and heard a sea hissing down. That was all there was time to hear, for suddenly I was choking in a torrent of foaming water; there seemed to be tons of it, all dark green and frothing, pushing me down. It seemed like hours before I surfaced. I had swallowed a great deal of water, as I always panic under water, and immediately the thought filled my waterlogged brain: 'If this is drowning, I don't like it.'

Bill and I were both still in the boat, now both on the port side, and still under the cover, so *Wanderer* must have rolled completely over – possibly several times. The mast crutch had gone, but that seemed all. I was still clutching the log. We bailed like hell, but there was not so much water as I had expected; probably the cockpit cover had kept a lot out. We pulled in the sea-anchor warp and discovered that it had broken near the clip. I went forward to tie on a small running drogue – an unpleasant task, but a skipper's job in such conditions.

The seas were enormous, rearing 30ft (9.14m) above us, with heavy water collapsing from each crest. I told Bill to get out the oil, but we found it had little effect. Possibly only 50 gallons (227.3 litres) at a time could hope to kill such seas. I got out a haversack to make a temporary drogue; Bill emptied the other rucksack and, by cutting holes in it, threaded them on to the shaft of the grapnel. We were only just in time, as the running drogue had now gone. Bill surged the new one, trying to keep us head on to the seas. I paused for a few seconds to admire the wild scene, and then we decided that we must have a larger drogue, and quickly. Fortunately the mainsail was still rolled round the boom – that could be used as a drogue, if I put a lashing on one end so that the sail opened into a cone when pulled through the water. Bill suggested that we doubled the warps. What a good idea! We should have done that before.

Working under the cover, I felt fear – if we capsized, I drowned! By uncleating the end of the warp, doubling it and attaching it by a bowline to the mainsheet, which I had already tied securely along the boom, we made ready. It was a risky operation to go forward to lead the ropes through the fair lead, as we now had no lifelines.

Our mainsail drogue worked well. Bill surged it, while I scrambled forward again to bring in the haversack. Not a hope in hell if I get swept off the bows! We badly needed our lifelines. The weight of the grapnel anchor was causing our bags to sink too deep, pulling our bows down into the breaking crests; so I pulled it in, removed the grapnel, shackled a short chain through the holes in the haversack with an empty tin of Shell oil on a 6ft (2m) line as a float, and once overboard it performed beautifully.

At 2345 a sea roared in from port and Wanderer *was rolled over again.* Winston Megoran.

We started a 15-minute watch system. Each in turn sat on the stern locker with the cockpit cover held round his waist, and pulled the dinghy into any crest that looked like becoming dangerous. It was very wet, very hard, work. Bill emptied the water with a bucket down to the floorboards during his watch and I crawled under the cockpit cover to pump out the rest. As I heard each wave roar down, I broke into a horrible sweat. It was an unpleasant, possibly fatal, position to be caught in if we capsized. Once the dinghy was pumped dry, I collected gloves from the underdeck bags and returned to the open air. The mast was dipping under the water as each wave caused the bow to lift, but it did not seem to be causing undue strain. I tried to doze, but it was quite impossible.

By 2015 it was Bill's watch and the seas were bad, at least 30ft (9.14m) and very heavy. Suddenly a real bad one roared down on us from the port side, and crashed in. Roaring right over us, it rolled us over. I had a fleeting memory of being thrown clean out of the stern, seeing Bill going under me, then the boat coming down on me. Down I went into the green depths with tremendous weight driving me downwards. More panic – down, down! Needing to breathe, I choked and began to drown.

We both surfaced clear of the boat and ropes, although Bill had the drogue warps over his head and shoulders. He climbed over the dinghy stern, but I lacked the strength to do the same. So I hooked an arm and leg over one side and rolled in as *Wanderer* rolled towards me. The boat was completely full. Bill took the warps forward through the fair leads and began to surge the dinghy. He had to keep his head up at all costs. If he was seasick now, he would lose his strength and determination, and those were the only two things that would keep him alive in these conditions. So I bailed with the bucket and felt dreadful.

The mast had gone, the centre section of it shattered for about 5ft (1.52m) of its length and its top banging into the side of the boat, only held by the halyards and splintered wood. I was about to cut it adrift by severing the shrouds, when Bill suggested that we ought to keep it. 'We may want it tomorrow,' he suggested dryly. Just then I was more concerned about riding out the gale. Conditions were far worse than I had imagined. However, I undid the shrouds from the hound band and pushed the shattered wooden mess beneath the cover.

The seas became even worse, and much more confused with a heavy cross sea building up as the wind backed. I would have felt frightened had there been time to think. I wondered if we would be alive to see the morning, and felt surprised that I was not particularly worried at the thought we might not.

The cover was keeping most of the water out of the boat, for the seas seemed to wash straight over it and one merely had to lift the cover to let the water run back to where it belonged. It was only necessary to bail when a heavy sea came aboard – about every 10 minutes.

It was now quite impossible to look into the wind. It was screaming, and the tops of the waves were blown completely away, hitting one's body, and feeling like hail. Within our limited vision the whole sea seemed to be smoking. Entire waves were breaking in a wall of solid water with tremendous roars. Just to see such seas breaking away on the beam was frightening – 25ft (7.62m) of solid water, with another 12ft (3.66m) of overhanging crest above it. It was only a matter of time before we got one aboard. It was impossible for such a little boat to rise to it; even a five-tonner would have been driven under.

We continued to surge the warps in 10 minutes. It became difficult to see through my glasses. My cleaning handkerchief was saturated, so I kept wiping my gloved finger over the lens, which at least spread the salt evenly – sufficient for me to see anyway.

About 2100 hours we caught the inevitable. I just had time to shout to Bill. We both hauled in on the warps frantically, attempting to pull *Wanderer* through the crest. She rose gallantly, but was in an impossible position: she seemed to be rising at 60° and there was still a 15ft (4.57m) crest curling above us. Down it came and we were driven bodily under. With ears roaring under tremendous pressure, and swallowing water, I fought back to the surface, only to discover that *Wanderer* was lying bottom up. I had visualised this happening. Now we must find the answer quickly if we were to survive. The boat would be very stable in that position, especially with the rollers tied in the bilges.

I found myself at the stern, and pulled myself round to the same side as Bill, and we climbed aboard. It was a bit difficult with waterlogged clothes and boots full of water, but the bilge runner just gave us a toe hold, and we were able to jam our fingers in the centreboard slot. I noticed that the self-bailer was not sealing properly – no wonder the boat had leaked. We must have done the damage unloading her at Kinlochbervie. With the help of the next wave we were able to roll *Wanderer* over. We climbed in and found her full of water, right to the very top of the rear buoyancy, and waves continued to wash in. The drogue lines had jumped out of the fair lead and, telling Bill to keep his head up, I asked him to lead the warps forward. I could not find our buckets beneath the cover, but with Mrs Jespersen's fish bucket and our plastic potty we both began to bail. Three times waves washed straight over us and refilled the boat, then just as we had become almost buoyant, another wave filled us. I heard myself scream out: 'Oh God! Give us a chance; we haven't cleared the last lot yet!' He gave us that chance, and we took it. Bill hauled in on the warps, to swing *Wanderer* head on to the seas, and held the cover over us, and I bailed flat out. The port rear floorboard had moved forward, so I had a bailing well. There is a lot of water in a waterlogged Wayfarer, but eventually I won.

At 2345 I shouted: 'Bill, the boat is completely dry, I shall be damned annoyed if you fill it again.' That was the wrong thing to have said, because immediately a sea roared in from port and *Wanderer* was rolled over. Once again I remember being thrown clear, Bill going under me, and the hull coming over on top. Again came the ghastly descent into dark green water, feeling the horrible weight over me and choking back to the surface. *Wanderer* lay on her side this time. We climbed aboard to find only 3in (7.62cm) of water in her. Most extraordinary! She must have rolled very quickly. We were very tired, especially mentally, and there was a constant roar, the sting of spray and the strain of judging each wave. The clouds began to clear slightly to the north, but the wind was as strong as ever. If the wind did not die down before darkness fell we should be in real trouble, for we should no longer be able to see the dangerous crests in time to pull the dinghy round to meet them bows on!

It was still pitch black at 0030 hours on Wednesday, the following day. The wind was still at full strength, and the seas as bad, if not worse, with heavy confused cross seas roaring about. I was shivering violently above deck, so I went below and was warmer, but the mental strain was too much to bear, with the possibility of being trapped under the cover if we capsized. Bill also kept sheltering and then emerging – I assume for the same reason.

We were hungry, but could find no food. It started to rain, but it would need a torrent to kill the sea. By 0130 it was just light enough to see, and there seemed to be a slight reduction in the wind – now about Force 8, and only occasionally gusting to 9. We were so cold that it took conscious thought to realise the difference in wind strength. The seas were still awe inspiring, and we were not yet out of trouble, but my brain was now ticking over and beginning to measure our chances. I now believed that we might survive – the boat was in good condition, and nothing essential was damaged; the drogues were working well, and showed every sign of lasting out; and the crew were both in good shape. I was amazed at Bill's stamina. He had not been sick during the storm, showed no signs of failing and was in better spirits than a few days ago.

The mast had shattered halfway along its length at the worst possible place, so that neither half was long enough to use on its own.

The broken ends were badly splintered and we had no spare wood to repair the spar. The mainsail, which was acting as a temporary drogue, was recoverable, provided the warps did not part; and even if it did carry away or was torn, we could manage with the two jibs, supposing they were still with us. All our water was still aboard, for the lashing had held during the previous night. Our food position was doubtful, since the tins had been emptied on to the floorboards when the rucksacks had been utilised as drogues, and had now probably all gone overboard. Perishable food in the under-deck bags must be ruined, but fortunately our eggs were still in stock, clipped in plastic containers beneath the decks.

The clouds were breaking up in the northern half of the horizon, from the west round to the north east, but that did not necessarily mean the end of the gale. There could be more to come. It was to be hoped not, for we needed warmth and sleep badly. I was not sure how many more capsizes we could survive – one, possibly two perhaps.

By dawn the wind was Force 8 and definitely moderating. A few hours more of this and the seas would have subsided. It was still much too dangerous to leave the dinghy to her own devices, and we continued working the warps, swinging her to meet each breaking sea. It was bitterly cold, and we were both shivering violently. I tried sitting on the water containers under the cover thus getting my body under cover but keeping my head in the open, but the water ran up my legs and pocketed around my thighs. I worked the water down past my knees and into my boots, and felt warmer. I felt sick with the salt water I had swallowed, and when Bill passed me a water container, I drank deeply.

At 0430 hours it was full daylight. The seas were as high as ever, but the wind was no more than Force 7. Mostly the seas were now breaking on the back face. Occasionally we shipped a green one, but fortunately they did not capsize us. I still could not relax and was desperately tired. An hour later the seas were still as bad, but the wind was dropping to Force 6. Bill was still working like a trouper, his strength never failing. Suddenly I realised that the worst was over, and felt completely drained of energy. I was bemused and numb with the reaction. We badly needed food.

13

Repairs

There was a ship of about 2,000 tons (2,032 tonnes) a mile to port, heading for Norway. Bill agreed that we were disabled and should accept help if we could attract attention. I was about to crawl under the cover for the Very pistol, but Bill had already passed me a white flare. Convinced that it would be invisible in the heavy seas and the daylight, but not wishing to hurt Bill's feelings, I lit it, but it burnt out and I scrambled for the flare box. Surprisingly it was still in position. I stripped off the pvc wrappings and fired a red flare, and then three more at approved 30-second intervals. We were now on the ship's quarter, and hoped that their lookout was awake. Bill steadied me while I stood up. I thought I could see a signal from the ship and fired two more cartridges. The signal turned out to be a petrel soaring above the ship. I fired one more cartridge, but there was no reply.

Bill took this failure to attract attention very well, but I felt very lonely. The seas were still running at 30ft (9.14m), but they no longer looked so dangerous. Bill continued to work, surging the drogue warps. His determination was amazing. Soon my gloves were worn right through the palm and fingers, and after that the ropes cut straight into my hands. The noise and ferocity of the seas still battered our senses, but I considered that we should be unlucky to capsize again.

Possibly we were the only people alive to have taken an open dinghy through a Force 9 gale, but we felt no elation, just a reaction of wetness, coldness and extreme tiredness. The cover had saved our lives.

Would these seas never go down? By 0830 I considered turning in. We continued half-hour watches, as the crew still had to haul *Wanderer*'s bows through the worst crests. At 0900 hours I was off duty, and I slept. At 0940 I began hauling through the waves again.

Bill had let me sleep an extra 10 minutes, bless him! We continued our watches until noon, and then both turned in. At 1330 hours I thought it safe to change out of our sodden clothing, without getting too wet. We had taken no sea aboard for 40 minutes, although the waves were still over 10ft (3.05m) high.

We shared what clothes we had left, mainly light shore-going garments and used clothing we had discarded days before as too damp to wear. I had one pair of wool pants and vest (used), one short vest (cotton), one Norwegian jersey, one padded jacket, and one jersey (loaned by Bill). Bill dressed in pyjama trousers, one pair of short pants, one pair of jeans (used), one vest (used), one shirt (used), two jerseys, and one anorak (used). We wrung out our socks, and

'After eighteen hours of lying to the drogue and four capsizes in Force 9 it was a relief when the seas died down and we could inspect the damage.' Surprisingly the Admiralty Pilot book, charts, sextant and other contents of the rear buoyancy locker were still dry!

found even in those conditions that it was a relief to change. However, our clothing was quite inadequate, and we should be suffering before we landed in Norway.

It was necessary to check our stores, re-rig and then sleep, though I am not sure that Bill agreed with the order of priority. We had 2½ gallons (11.36 litres) of water in three separate containers. The oven was torn away from its mountings under the seat and washed forward but the petrol stove from inside it had completely disappeared, but I had a spare petrol stove in the forward buoyancy, and I could see a mess tin in the shambles up forward. We had one haversack half full of reasonably balanced food, enough for three days at full rations. Two boxes of eggs were still in place, clipped under the side decks, which gave us twenty-four eggs or five meals. All our other tins had gone overboard. Still, we were not too badly fixed. We needed food for seven days to be safe.

The mast was the worst worry, seemingly beyond repair. I lifted the floorboards one by one, hoping to recover some stores from the bilges. While removing the pump in order to clean it, I found two tins of self-heating malted milk and one tin of crab. Under the rear floorboards there were two sets of cutlery, so cooking and eating could be taken care of.

Later I found another tin of self-heating soup and a tin of ham. The tools had gone – two sets of files and drills – and also the oilskin-repair kit, which would be serious if our waterproofs sprung a leak before we landed. Fortunately a coping saw and blades were still with us. All the necessary charts were present even if decidedly damp, and we still had the cine camera and films. When Bill bailed out the stern locker, we only found 2½ pints (1.42 litres) of water in it.

We considered the mast. We needed something to carry the full height of the genoa, but both ends of the mast were badly splintered for 6ft (1.83m). Deciding to use the bowsprit for a front splint and the remainder of the mast crutches for side splints, we notched the spars to prevent lashings slipping, and lashed them as firmly as we could manage with the burgee line. The repaired spar looked reasonable, but it was shattered for too great a length to expect any real strength – there was an open gap of 6in (15.24cm) in one place. I felt so much more cheerful that I got out toothbrush and paste to brush my teeth.

What a pleasure it was to remove five days' fur from one's mouth! I felt a new man. I noticed Bill had been pointing a camera at me and grinning, but I did not care. It was wonderful to be alive.

By 2100 hours with wind Force 2 westerly and the swell a mere 7ft (2.13m), we put up the genoa and set off due east for Stadt, 190 miles (305.59km) away. We heated a meal, and it went down well. Later Bill turned in and I took the first watch. I felt much happier to be under way again and sailing. An hour later the moon came up on our bows, and I had something to steer for. It was a memorable evening's sail, as I sailed straight down the path of the moon, soaking up the beauty of the sea and putting the unpleasant experiences of the last 24 hours back into focus.

We seemed to be moving slowly, with southerly winds, Force 2–3, and I hoisted the main, deep-reefed, hoping that the mast would take it. At the midnight forecast everything went wrong. I backed the jib and tied the tiller to loo'ard and *Wanderer* sat back gently. There were two minutes to go to the forecast when suddenly the jib sheet jam cleat let go, the genoa flogged madly, the lashing jumped off the tiller and the boat spun round. Bill shouted up to ask if he could do anything, and got snarled at for his pains. I grabbed the jib sheet and recleated them, then secured them to the thwarts. I relashed the tiller and got to the earphones just too late. I had missed the forecast except for 'Goodnight, gentlemen'.

The seas were increasing to white horses and we began to roll heavily. At 0030 on Thursday, the following day, I handed over to Bill after lowering the main. We were now broad reaching steadily towards the beautiful silver disc of the moon some 10° above the horizon, and going 4 knots under jib alone. Once below, I immediately fell into a deep sleep. At 0100 something was wrong. I made a real effort to climb back to consciousness. The mast had gone. Bill was shouting for help to get it down. Suddenly the fact penetrated, and I snapped awake. Bill told me later that I awoke swearing fearfully. The top half of the mast was leaning drunkenly forward at an angle of 25° under the pull of the jib. It was essential to get it down before it broke, otherwise we could lose all our splints and lashings, of which we were desperately short. Disconnecting the jib hanks, we got the mast down, and because it whipped into the sea every wave we rose to, we removed the tabernacle pin and tied down the mast to the foredeck and mainsheet horse, with a roller beneath to prevent chafe.

We stowed the dinghy for the night, and put out our kit-bag anchor. Thoroughly cold and wet, I removed my socks, wrung them out and felt a little better. I suggested that we rigged the two headcovers and sleep with our heads under the foredeck, but Bill vetoed the suggestion. He had visions of another capsize and wanted his head in the open air. We untied the storm cover, pulled it half over us, inflated the lilos and turned in. It was too dark to repair the mast and in any case the sea was too rough.

At 0900 hours I woke shivering with cold, to find the boat was sliding sideways and rolling heavily. Getting up to inspect, I found the seas much worse than last night, but by 1400 they were better and it was just possible to work on the mast. I called Bill, who looked very bad. We both needed sleep, food and warmth, but I was obsessed by the need to get the mast repaired and the boat rigged. We could sleep later under way. Exercise would warm Bill, too, so I drove him to work; he must have hated the sight of me just then.

We removed the splints and lashings and then we heard aircraft engines! I got out my Very pistol, just in case, but was not sure that I should use it, as I did not want to start an international search. Bill did not agree; he was still suffering from reaction from the Force 9, whereas I was recovering. The aircraft was well above the cloud ceiling, so it saved any argument.

Our files (flat and round), pliers, drills and screwdrivers had all gone overboard, but we had the coping saw. That was a godsend, for work with a knife would have been much slower. After much discussion, we adopted Bill's ideas for repairing the mast. The hound band and shrouds were moved to the mast head for more support. Bill measured up and worked out how much of the splintered centre section we could remove and still get a full hoist of genoa. The coping saw blade broke and, while fitting a new one, I felt desperately cold and began shivering. Bill looked even worse than I felt. The new blade sliced through the wood, revealing an excellent mast section. I doubt if many dinghy sailors see a section of their own masts while they are afloat.

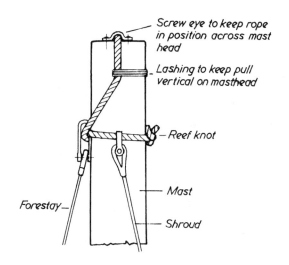

Jury rig, showing lashing for forestay and shrouds.

We offered up the ends of the mast by inserting the ensign staff in the luff groove, and fitted the splints as before. When we tightened up the lashings, we found that the splints tended to move forward – probably the cause of the mast collapsing the night before. We needed distance pieces to prevent this happening again. The jib stick was the only packing piece suitable, so I cut it up. We removed all the lashings, and I offered up the splints and bamboo packing while Bill put on the lashings again. He had to unravel some terylene rope, as cord was very short, but it looked a good workman-like job. I fitted lashings to the mast head in a figure of eight by a lashing eye screwed to the crown of the mast. The pull of the shrouds would tighten the strap on the mast head, and ensure that the pull was kept directly downwards.

At 2000 hours (an hour earlier than the previous night – we must be improving!) we put up the mast. Bill suggested a good night's sleep before we set sail, but I overruled him, so that we should use the fair wind. However, we both agreed to hail any passing trawler heading for Norway.

Up genoa, wind Force 4 south west, and we set up a steady 4 knots. I cooked a meal of meat and vegetables. At 2100 Bill turned in.

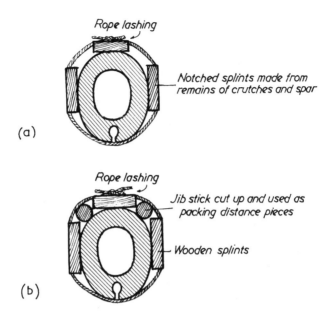

Rope lashing

Notched splints made from
remains of crutches and spar

(a)

Rope lashing

Jib stick cut up and used as
packing distance pieces

Wooden splints

(b)

Mast repair after Force 9: first repair (a) was unsatisfactory owing to length of splintered mast and tendency of splints to move forward and loosen under strain; second repair (b) was sound and capable of windward work. All splintered wood was cut out and the distance pieces fitted between splints prevented them moving forward.

I doubt that he could have slept, for he was too tired and still suffering from shock, and it was noisy below with the waves slamming the hull.

Personally I felt happy and contented. *Wanderer* was mobile, the crew was in good health, we had food and water and now a rig that could stand a hard beat off the coast if necessary. I wished we had more line, so that we could have added another couple of lashings to the mast.

A small trawler came up out of the south west, heading for Iceland. I could see the helmsman looking at us intently, but I pretended I did not see him, and after some hesitation the ship steamed off. I was not sure about Bill's reaction, but I did not want to be rescued now.

Our speed increased, as did the wind. I doubted if Bill could sleep with the dinghy surfing into each trough. At 2300 he came on duty, looking done in, but I hardened my heart. If we once began to feel sorry for ourselves, we should relax, go to pieces, and begin to suffer from exhaustion and exposure.

My mental estimate was that we were about 150 miles (241.39km) west of Stadt, and possibly a little north as well. We therefore went on to a bearing of 110°. We could rely on finding shelter on one side or the other of Stadt.

My legs and thighs were trembling with cold, and so I removed Bill's loaned jersey and used it instead as a pair of pants. I looked everywhere in the boat for a bar of Horlick's rum fudge as an encouragement for Bill, but it had all gone overboard.

At 0100 on the following day, Friday, I came on duty never having felt colder. It had been impossible to sleep, owing to the constant banging. Bill said it was blowing up again, and he wanted to lay to a drogue until daylight. Since he was almost at the end of his tether, I agreed, and we took down the sail and laid out our rucksack sea anchor. *Wanderer* rolled heavily, almost shaking the mast out of the boat each time a shroud tightened, until I decided that we must hoist a small jib and continue sailing, otherwise all the lashings would shake loose. Poor Bill, no sleep again! I stowed the drogue and the boat lay quietly, drifting in the right direction, so we both turned in until dawn.

It was daylight at 0400 and bitterly cold. My feet were like blocks of ice, so I removed my boots, squeezed out my socks, and changed the wettest pair for some discarded five days ago as unwearable. I offered Bill some hot malted milk, which he refused, saying that he did not like it. Pedantically I told him that to stay alive we needed warmth, and since his clothing was insufficient, he must eat whatever he was given *and keep it down*! He grinned, and the malted milk disappeared.

Up genoa and off at 3 knots, wind south west, Force 3. One lashing on the jury rig had worked loose, but everything else had held well. At 0645 I called Bill for the shipping forecast but he got nothing on the radio set, and so he steered while I made a meal. I hoped to get a noon sight but the sun disappeared at 1100 hours. I hoped to take a radio fix later. At 1340 I called Bill to steer while I took a noon sight. He tried heaving to, but the boat rolled heavily, and had to sail along the wave crests to give me a longer time to take the sight. The first sight of 45° 49′ remained constant for 15 minutes, and then the sun dropped behind the clouds. Here are my calculations:

Noon Sight Friday

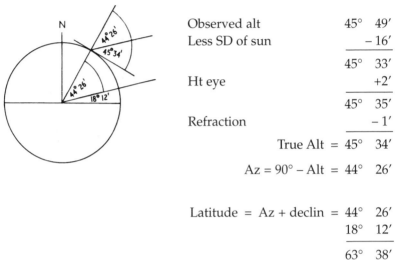

Observed alt	45°	49′
Less SD of sun		– 16′
	45°	33′
Ht eye		+2′
	45°	35′
Refraction		– 1′
True Alt =	45°	34′
Az = 90° – Alt =	44°	26′

Latitude = Az + declin =	44°	26′
	18°	12′
	63°	38′

Latitude 63° 38′ surprised me, for we were some 90 miles (144.84km) north of our expected position. Feeling doubtful, I did a DF radio fix.

294	GY	– – . , – . – –		
294	BJ	– . . . , . – – –	255° magnetic	
379	LIF	. – . . , . . , . . – .	310°	″
		– –	350°	″

NB Aircraft beacon position only approx on chart.

The radio fix put us 90 miles south of the sun sight and agreed with the estimated position. Suddenly I realised I must have made mistakes in my geometry and checked back:

Observed alt	45°	49'
Plus SD of sun		16'
	46°	5'
Ht eye		– 2'
	46°	3'
Refraction		– 1'
True altitude	46°	2'
Az	= 43°	58'

Latitude = Az + declin =	43°	58'
	18°	12'
	62°	10'

The second results were much better. I had made several errors the first time, (1) subtracting the sun's semi-diameter, instead of adding, and (2) making an error of 1° in addition. All three positions – RDF, DR, and noon sight – now agreed.

We were approximately 55 miles (88.51km) offshore, and had made better time than I had expected, probably because of surface drift in the bad weather plus the influence of the Gulf Stream. Bill asked me about my homework, and when I explained my errors, he told me any educated monkey could have done as well, and that he was surprised I had ever managed to hit Norway at all. I enjoyed my watch.

14

The Norwegian Coast

We suddenly realised that we could be ashore tomorrow. This would be my fourth crossing to Norway, and I had much to do. I wanted to visit the Seljestokkens, whom I had met on a previous trip to Norway, but their farm was to windward of Stadt, and I felt Aalesund was the easier landfall, being further down wind. Besides, I wanted to attend service again in the beautiful parish church there. I would have to fly home to be at work on the following Saturday, and I also wanted to visit Mr Ellingsen and his wife Else, in Bergen, and the Aarnots in Molde, for they had all been good to me on previous cruises to their beautiful country, but even with a good mast, there would not be time, as they lived 30 miles (48.28km) beyond Aalesund.

A squall swept across the southern horizon, giving us torrential rain. Bill made a sandwich from the tin of crab meat. By now our hands were so swollen and tender that it was difficult to open tins or hold anything. I took out the jersey that Mrs Jespersen had presented to me in the Faeroes – it had been safe, with Bill's, in the forward buoyancy compartment. It was meant to be worn on special occasions only, but necessity came first. I turned in very sleepy, and almost warm, and only stayed awake long enough to write up my personal log. I fell asleep with my hands inside my oilskins and tucked under my armpits for warmth, which was a mistake for when Bill called me out of a dead sleep, my hands had dried out and warmed up. They hurt me worse than any hotache I had ever experienced. My good sleep had set up a reaction, and I felt exhausted and drained of all will power. I suggested that Bill heated a meal. He felt dreadful and I felt worse, and an argument almost started up. So I cooked the evening meal. It was Scotch broth and beef curry. Bill disapproved of the mixture, but we both felt better after swallowing the hot slush.

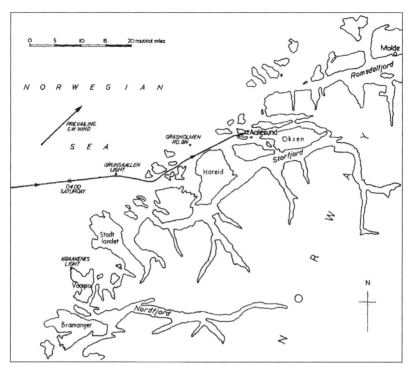

Bill said that he thought he had seen land 40 minutes before, then together we saw a flash of light 25° on the starboard bow. Land! It was too far away to time the light, but essential that we got a bearing to enable us to come in north of Stadt; the land sloped away north-eastwards, and if we were caught in a south-west gale, we would have extra sea-room. The weather seemed settled, but this was the part of cruising I liked least – closing the land. The mast would stand some close-hauled work if we had to claw offshore, but we ought not to put more strain on it than necessary.

I settled down to sailing again. Lights were occasionally flashing on the bows and others on our starboard. The one ahead was probably Stadt, and the one slightly to port possibly Grundskallen. We could not check the flashes yet, as the range was too great and the seas too big. However, I got out the coastal chart of this area and folded it ready.

On Saturday at 0200 I handed over to Bill and told him to head for the light I presumed to be Grundskallen (2 flashes, 30 seconds). I decided I would check the times later, and turned in, my top half pleasantly warm, but my bottom half shivering. I slept well. When I woke the wind was south west, Force 2, and a lighthouse on our bows only 5 miles (8.05km) away, and the headland of Stadtlandet black and brooding was away on our starboard beam. I recognised both from a previous cruise. We were almost in sheltered water, and it was quite a relief to be safely clear of a rotten lee shore. We were doing 3 knots under genoa.

Bill said that a Shell tanker had headed for us at dawn. He thought it was going to run us down, but the skipper merely waved and departed. I opened a tin of self-heating malted milk but it would not light, the first dud one we had had. The next one did ignite, and it was our last one. Mist covered everything, and the coast and island disappeared completely, but we had taken an accurate bearing on the lighthouse. The wind suddenly jumped into SSE, and we could just lay our course. Gradually our speed dropped to 1 knot, and *Wanderer* sagged away. Before putting up the mainsail, I needed a shot of Bill looking exhausted to complete the cine film, so I woke him from a deep sleep and got the ideal picture. He was very bolshy and turned in much aggrieved. Taking a cine film in extreme conditions was not the way to keep one's friends.

I put up the main, which did not set too badly except that the luff stood away from the mast 9in (22.86cm) at the top. Our speed increased, and we entered a tide rip. The chart was already marked up with courses and distances through the fjords to Aalesund from a previous cruise, although I did cut between the islands to shorten the distance.

The scenery was wonderful – a valley between the mountains with clouds hanging on to the peaks, golden in the morning sun. I almost woke Bill to enjoy it, but thought that he would disapprove of being woken again during his off watch. I sailed alongside an outboard dinghy pulling in cod to ask the fisherman if we could get through a narrow gut between the islands to Aalesund. The answer was 'Ya'. Bill awoke on hearing voices, turned over and went to sleep again.

Passing the islands, I sailed into the next fjord where we were overtaken by a fishing boat, which offered us a tow, but it was

Opposite: Arrival in Aalesund under jury rig after the rough passage.

turning down a side fjord, so I thanked the crew and declined. They noticed our red ensign and asked us if we had crossed Nordsjoen. I replied 'Ya', to which they said, 'You are madmans', and I think they meant it, too.

The wind slowly died to Force 1 southerly, and we had a long drift down the fjord. When Bill awoke, I took a cine shot of him steering with mountains and villages in the background. Rounding the last headland, we approached Aalesund, sailed into the harbour and tied *Wanderer* up, and climbed on to the public quay. Both of us had difficulty in not falling down, as we had lost our land legs. People soon collected, and somebody took us to buy some clothes and shoes. Both shops were shut, but they opened specially. We must both have looked dreadful, with rough uncombed hair, ten days' beard badly matted, and eyes gummed up with salt. We must have smelt worse than we looked, but the Grand Hotel admitted us without question as soon as they knew we were English. Our first request was for a bath and a shave. We wrote a few postcards and then slept. The hotel staff were very kind – a waitress noticed my raw hands and gave me some handcream and insisted I used it while she watched. Normally I would not touch the stuff for fear of appearing effeminate.

Bill decided that he had to leave on the next afternoon's passenger ship to Bergen, and thence to England as he had to see his sister off to America and also wanted to varnish his Finn mast in time for the Finn Olympic trials for Tokyo as he was hoping to be chosen to go over with the British team. I was sorry he had to go, because I had hoped we might sail a little further to Kristiansund. However, we should be able to attend morning service together before he went.

On the Sunday morning I awoke early from habit, to find it was blowing a Force 7 gale from the south west. Thankfully I tucked my burning hands beneath my armpits and went straight back to sleep, slightly irritated that the bed would not keep still. I awoke again at 0600 and felt it was time to be on watch, but laid in bed enjoying the warmth. Hands and feet hurt badly.

Breakfast was enjoyable. I had forgotten the pleasures of a Norwegian breakfast, with the many cold dishes of various fish and meats. We made absolute pigs of ourselves.

Bill and I went to the dinghy to pack the gear he needed, and then walked to the parish church of Aalesund. We enjoyed the service, which was Lutheran and very close to our own Church of England ceremonies. After lunch I walked to the steamer quay with Bill, both of us feeling rather depressed, as it was the end of our holiday. Bill had been a first-rate crew, and I was sorry to see him leave. At the ship Bill realised that he had forgotten some gear. I tore back to *Wanderer* at full stretch, and a taxi driver gave me a lift back but would not accept payment.

Afterwards I stopped at the shipping office to say thank you to the manager, Mr Aslak Solbjerg, and we stopped to chat. He then drove me back to the hotel.

I wanted to sail on to Molde or Kristiansund very badly, and thought that I could manage singlehanded in sheltered water between the islands. However, the snags were a suspect rig and no dry clothes. Also I had to complete the Shell film and that would take time to organise, in fairness to Shell. There was plenty to film in Norway. Mr Solbjerg called to see me with a reporter, and we adjourned to his home. A promise was made that I would later be invited back for a meal of whale meat, which I had always wanted to try.

The following morning in the hotel I again ate a solid breakfast of sild, herring, eel, halibut, cheese, goat cheese, cereals, smoked sausage, and sliced meats, and returned for more portions of the superb mackerel and fresh milk. A radio commentator called me to ask if there was anything I needed, and to book an interview later that morning.

At the radio station I enjoyed the chat with Mr Ronneberg, the person in charge of the radio interview. He was peculiarly reluctant to talk about himself, and I learnt later that he had been decorated for his part in the war. After I had done the interview, Mr Solbjerg was waiting outside the building to ask me to join his family for dinner, as his wife had prepared 'Whalebif'. He also drove me out to see the Viking Natural History Museum. I was also keen to visit a Viking village set in a valley, but it was closed. Back at the hotel Mr Ronneberg phoned me from the radio station, asking me to dine with him and his family. He also mentioned that he had arranged for the Viking village museum to be opened for me. What a clash of engagements! I was sorry not to be able to accept both invitations, but the whale meat was delicious, and the evening with the Solbjerg family much appreciated. I learnt that the local papers, reporting our cruise, made it sound a little hair-raising. On reflection it did seem incredible that boat and crew should have survived. We were told later that the summer had been the worst for over a century.

I have always picked my cruising area with care – any area with a record of gales was avoided like the plague. Even in the NE Atlantic, which is known as a robust area, gales of Force 8 in the summer are infrequent. The Norwegian Sea should have been easier. It was unfortunate that the one year that we chose to cruise from Faeroes to North Norway was the worst year in over a century and included two Force 9s – and we caught one of them. The offshore sailor must be prepared to take whatever the sea throws at him. It reminded me of Bill Jacob's comment 'the sea has no favourites' and '. . . if you get into trouble you must be prepared to get yourself out of it by your own efforts'.

An offshore lifeboat stationed with the fishing fleet towed a trawler in from Faeroe a couple of days later, and the first mate could not believe we had crossed safely in the recent weather.

PART V

THE LAST WORD
BY MARGARET DYE

The Last Word
by Margaret Dye

I have read in authoritative sailing magazines that Frank has been described alternately as 'a madman of the Atlantic' and 'a legend in his own time'.

What caused such extreme comments are the offshore dinghy cruises Frank planned from the 1960s onwards with a variety of male crew. Over the years I read about these adventures with excitement and envy. Eventually I met Frank at a local sailing course, where he was an invited lecturer and I a student.

'Don't sail with that man, he'll kill you,' said my sailing tutor, overhearing Frank's invitation for me to sail in *Wanderer* in the Wash the following Sunday.

The happiest and most hellish times in my life have been when crewing in *Wanderer*, and I am proud and content that she now lives in the National Maritime Museum, Cornwall. That beautiful and enthusiastic museum provides her with an interesting retirement as she is surrounded by a changing and developing fleet of historic boats.

Maybe I should have been warned: when discussing our future plans, Frank said, 'You can sail anywhere you like for our honeymoon'. Enthusiastically I replied, 'We'll take *Wanderer* to Venice and sail to art galleries, palaces and concerts and sleep afloat in the lagoons'. The subject was not mentioned again, but a year later we set off to St Kilda, launching from Skye. The fact that Frank had a very inexperienced crew did not affect his plans. His optimism and adaptable attitude overcame all my inexperience – like nearly capsizing in the dark in the turbulent Minch because I steered for the masthead light of a trawler which I mistook for the star I was sailing by. I soon learnt how adaptable Frank was when we attempted to leave Port o' Ness two days after our landfall at Butt of Lewis from St Kilda. With nearly gale force stern winds and turbulent seas all the

Downwind sailing with jib and genoa goosewinged.

way from America, and with deep reefed mainsail and storm jib we had a hard time preventing *Wanderer* from broaching, so Frank put back to the island to experiment with *Wanderer*'s rig. We set out for a second time carrying a jib and genoa goosewinged on the forestay, all the way across the Minch. 'The old square riggers running in the Roaring Forties used to rig a canvas behind the helmsman to prevent him seeing the mountainous waves rolling up astern and then leaving the wheel in fright and the ship broaching,' Frank explained encouragingly. 'I read about it years ago.'

On land Frank appears to me to be shy, even inarticulate; I don't think he is completely happy in today's society, and he is very dismissive when people in authority try to justify slack thinking and inefficiency. Once in a Wayfarer, however, he is happy and completely at home.

After many cruises in *Wanderer*, uppermost in the memory are times when we got caught out in the gap between the Shetlands and Fair Isle. The NW near-gale that came in was unforecast, and with wind against tide, the seas were unbelievable. In the dusk I watched Frank working round the boat, taking down the mast, unshipping the rudder and laying out the drogue. We watched the mountainous white foam-flecked waves roar past the boat and, thinking we could not survive long, I said, 'Which do you want, red or white?' knowing the flares were stored in the underdeck bag. Frank's reply calmed me down, 'You can't expect others to risk their lives; we came out here of our own free will.'

Years later *Wanderer* was taking us down a Norwegian fjord open to the sea. It was the end of our holiday and summer had turned to winter and once again I was frozen with cold. In the early days our cruising clothes were not sophisticated, as they are today. (We even wore rubber boots two sizes too large, so that they could be kicked off in the event of a capsize.) The forcast gale broke just as night approached; crouched on the thwarts, knowing there was no safe anchorage along this iron bound fjord, expecting to capsize as each white frothing wave roared beneath us, I watched Frank, calm and concentrated, relaxed but wary, enjoying the moment and extending his techniques.

Living with cold in a dinghy is a challenge, but nothing prepared me for the heat, humidity and extreme weather *Wanderer* met sailing northward from Miami. Watching Frank prepare for the forecast 'severe and damaging thunderstorms' as darkness fell was an exercise in restraint. The water was an oily calm and the forecaster warned, 'All boats should seek shelter'.

'What we need is a hurricane hole!' I muttered as I prepared supper, watching Frank lay out the anchors in a 'V' and row them in, set up a riding light and finally set up lightning conductors to the shrouds. I could not forget years earlier seeing the damage done to a GRP Wayfarer in the Canadian Great Lakes when a lightning strike had flashed down the shrouds and literally melted the hull. So we ate watching the vortexing clouds and lightning coming closer, cautiously wearing rubber boots and rubber gloves, with big yachts dragging their anchors and dragging down on us, and wondering what we could do if they fouled *Wanderer* . . .

Many miles further up the coast of America we tied *Wanderer* to the piles of the marina dinghy dock and, after visiting the Wooden Boat Show at Beaufort NC, we prepared lunch. It was to be a special feast to celebrate a good sail over recent days. Ripe melon slices and peeled shrimps were already laid out on the thwarts with the front of the tent rigged to shelter us from the searing heat. 'Look at that peculiar cloud seaward,' I remarked, as Frank completed laying out a stern anchor, and we began enjoying our melon. The light breeze suddenly erupted into a full Force 8 and within minutes waves were piling across the bay, the anchor dragged and we were pinned under the jetty.

'Get the tent off – quick,' shouted Frank. Seeing that he could scarcely hold *Wanderer* from being blown broadside under the jetty, I tore off the Velcro strips securing the tent to the hull and fell on it before it was blown overboard. Ten minutes later with the squall gone, we rowed across the creek, tied our bows to a pile, reset the stern anchor, rerigged the tent and rescued our meal from the bilges.

'We could easily have lost our mast,' Frank muttered. Several yachts were starting their engines, recovering their dragged anchors and resetting them round us as we dusted sand off the melon slices and shrimps.

Frank had many male crew in the early days of sailing offshore before I knew him, and usually after one cruise they were off on their

Margaret off duty.

own – still enjoying sailing. For years I have sailed with Frank, and am grateful for a lifetime of memories afloat, but Frank is a man apart, a fine seaman with enormous endurance. *Wanderer* has made us friends all over the world and provided us with the best adventures one could wish to remember: luckily the urgency to be afloat exploring quiet and secretive places has never left us. *Wanderer* remains our lifelong friend and energiser because long after the hardships have been forgotten, the peace, beauty and satisfactions of dinghy cruising remain a focal point in our lives. Frank continues to demonstrate his adaptability and the flexibility of dinghy sailing techniques. Using, as always, his engineering background, he recently built me an electric starter for my outboard that is light enough to use, as I can no longer pull the starting cord.

Perhaps it is worth mentioning the impression he made on an experienced Canadian sailor:

For some fifteen years I've been in contact by letter with the redoubtable Frank Dye, Mr Wayfarer Cruiser himself. And, like every other dinghy cruiser, I've followed his career in those famous books, seen that extraordinary film, read about him in magazines and newspapers and heard stories from people who have been Over 'Ome. Yet I have never met the man.

In August, during a Wayfarer cruise, several reports and growing rumours were circulating about Frank. We knew he had sailed, bit by bit, up the US east coast over a period of years, starting in Florida in 1988. August 1988 saw him in New York Harbour, the following year he sailed up to Maine, and in the summer the rumours were that he was attempting to sail from Portland, across the Bay of Fundy, round Nova Scotia, across the Gulf of the St Lawrence and up the Labrador coast . . . and all singlehanded! Speculation and questions abounded. How would he watch-keep at night? How would he cross the freighter lanes? Was he planning, perhaps, a crossing of the North Atlantic? And so on.

Two months later, my wife and I just happened to be on a trip down East. We read in a local newspaper that an English sailor in a tiny open sailing vessel had breezed into the Halifax Government

Dock the previous Thursday. By the time we got there we found that he'd quietly toddled off again (in awful weather) round to the Armbro YC and was tied up at a snug berth, living in the dinghy, touring Halifax on foot and making plans to close down for the winter.

We visited him in his newfangled Proctor Special where he was being unobtrusive, independent and self-sufficient. The Armbro YC had offered him the hospitality of warm, dry quarters but he preferred to stay in the dinghy. He told us that this year he had travelled, in fits and starts, by day-sailing up the coast from Portland in Maine, to Grand Manan, New Brunswick (where he encountered the red tape of Canada Customs). From there he negotiated Fundy tides, touched Yarmouth and continued day sailing, sometimes fogbound, up the coast of Nova Scotia until he got to Halifax.

He piloted with photocopied, Scotch-taped charts by the 'turn-left-at-the-next-headland' sort of sailing. Before the weather turned too cold he planned to sail back to La Have, near Bridgewater, where he had arranged to store the dinghy over the winter while he went home to the UK. Next year he hopes to return to cruise the Newfoundland coast. Typically, he didn't even mention how he would get across the hundred miles of the freighter-fraught, tidal-fierce and foggy Cabot Straight.

To meet him for the first time, Mr Wayfarer seems quite unlike one who has performed those extraordinary sailing feats. He's 60-ish, a bit absent-minded, has a stocky, youthful figure, wears baggy pants with pockets stuffed with notebooks, and has a startling shock of thick, white, wiry hair, beard and all, round an impish, bespectacled face. And the way he talks is like someone merely day-tripping from TS and CC to Toronto Islands. All very low-key and modest. That's Frank.

Ken Elliott
Toronto East Fleet Captain Report

APPENDIX A

Equipment and Techniques

Dinghy cruising in open water is safe – provided the crew are prepared to gain their experience slowly and are professional in their approach. There are dangers, of course, the two most important being a lee shore, and heavy weather, but with careful planning these risks can be reduced to an acceptable minimum.

There is a limit to the amount of heavy weather that any boat can stand. By reading of open boat voyages (whaleboats, Eskimo kayaks, ships, lifeboats, etc) I made some assumptions about the behaviour of an open boat like a Wayfarer in open water – this was before I started cruising – and these have proved reasonably accurate:

Force 7–8: with mast lowered into a crutch the boat should 'weathercock' laying to a sea-anchor, and with a cover over the cockpit should be quite safe; probable drift 1 knot.

Force 8 (gale): would be acceptable. Only the top 4ft (1.3m) of the waves break and the sea-anchor should pull the boat through these.

Force 8 gale backing (or veering) after blowing for some hours: this would build up a bad cross sea probably more than a dinghy could survive. An extreme test of the competence of the crew.

Crew

I have had many different crew on my various passages and invariably I have learned a great deal from them. Only Bob Wright, John Buckingham and Marg have cruised with me more than once – not, I hasten to add, because the others would not go again, but because they enjoyed it and were off cruising on their own. Marg has sailed with me on all my recent cruises – St Kilda, Denmark, and Northern Norway above the Arctic Circle – and an excellent crew she is.

It is not easy to specify what makes a good crew. A professional approach is essential – the amateurish attitude of 'it will be all right on the day' is no good at sea. The sea is dangerous and the penalty for failure is too high. Determination and self discipline are high on the list, and so are sound judgement, a willingness to do more than half the work, and a sense of humour. Some people have another quality and I am not even sure that I know what it is. Bill mentioned after the gale off the Faeroes that when he came almost to the end of his endurance his mind seemed to leave his body and became a calculating machine working with amazing speed and wonderful clarity assessing our chances and what needed to be done; his body was no more than a machine subservient to his mind which would go on working until something stopped it! I was too tired to think that comment through and dismissed it as part of Bill's rather warped sense of humour. Some time later Ken Jensen, a Danish Wayfarer friend (whose toughness belies his sophisticated appearance), mentioned having a similar experience in a tight corner and he said 'it was a very odd feeling'. I think perhaps it was what the Vikings called 'berserker'.

Watches

When sailing offshore during daylight we work a strict 3-hour watch system, and at night or in bad conditions this is reduced to 2 hours. In cold weather it is impossible to sleep for more than an hour until one toughens up. With strange conditions it is not possible to sleep deeply and efficiency decreases quickly until the crew become acclimatised. This does not take long, maybe 3 days or less in good weather. Bad weather at the beginning of a cruise is a real problem giving the crew little chance to settle easily into a routine and the resultant seasickness saps both strength and resolution. Aboard *Wanderer* the one on watch has the sole responsibility for the boat; he sails, reefs singlehanded, navigates, carries out any necessary maintenance, and makes his own decisions – and without waking his partner except in an emergency. It is, of course, necessary to wake him when tacking to meet a wind shift, for it is alarming to find oneself suddenly down to leeward in a heeling dinghy and the boat needs the live ballast moved to windward anyway. Apart from the unexpected wind shift we only change tack at the change of watch.

Lifelines

It is important to wear lifelines all the time, especially at night and in rough conditions. In a choppy sea with a swell running a man is virtually invisible at 75yd (70m); there could be the possibility of a capsize when working back to pick him up if the wind was squally; and there is no certainty of waking the sleeping member of the crew before the boat sails away out of earshot. I have always felt therefore that lifelines are preferable to lifejackets – at least you are still tethered to the boat! We attach our lines to the centre thwart as it is a very strong, and central, anchorage point. Lifelines should be at least 16ft (5m) long to reduce the possibility of getting caught up in the rigging in a capsize.

Clothing

Great changes have taken place in clothing since Marg and I taught ourselves how to sail. We have become so used to modern high-tech fabrics that an effort is needed to remember that wool was the standard material for sailing clothes (jerseys, underclothes, trousers, socks) being a good insulator when wet, with a fisherman's smock to keep the wind off. String vests were a recent innovation; oilskins (and sou'westers) were made of waxed canvas that stuck when folded and needed strength to unroll and put on; zips were unknown (everything was buttoned) and Velcro was a long way into the future. Lifejackets were enormously bulky (being made of cork or kapok) fitted around the waist and it was rumoured they would drown an unconscious man or break his neck if he jumped from any height. Dinghy sailors were beginning to use inflatable ex-RAF 'Mae Wests' as they became available in military surplus stores.

Wet suits are not practical for extended use as the skin cannot 'breathe' and soon goes white and dead looking – it was called 'trench foot' in the 1914–18 world war.

One-piece oilskins are essential for offshore work in an open boat. Storm cuffs at the wrist and elastic at the ankles prevent water leaks into the suit especially when lying down on the floorboards to sleep.

Warm feet and hands are important. We wore wellington boots two sizes too large to make room for extra socks, and in the event of a capsize they could be kicked off easily. We also wore oversize oilskins which enabled us, in cold weather, to withdraw our hands inside the elastic cuffs.

Clothing is now lighter, easier to don, more resistant to wear and abrasion and like wool retains 85% of its insulation properties when wet. I carried a set of 'Trax' cold weather clothing in *Wanderer* so long that I forgot where it was stowed. Eventually I needed it with the onset of a Canadian winter – and it was wonderful. A neck cloth to keep the water out and the warmth in, and a Scottish wool balaclava which could be rolled up or pulled down to the shoulders for insulation (the greatest loss of heat is from the head and shoulders) are essentials, for it is always cold on the temperate seas of northern Europe.

Buoyancy

We carry spare clothing in the stern buoyancy compartment together with sleeping bags, air beds, tent, charts and navigation equipment; and spare rudder blade, clothing, repair kit, rope, etc in the forward buoyancy; and even with these compartments virtually full the Wayfarer still has a great reserve of positive buoyancy. Two pneumatic rollers are lashed beneath the side benches and in addition to providing extra buoyancy they are excellent for rolling the boat up a steep beach, or back into the water, and they can also be hung alongside to act as fenders when in harbour.

Singlehanding

This has only one advantage – meeting local people is even easier.

Seasickness

This is an unpleasant, distressing illness. It has to be accepted as a fact of life by the sailors but it is also dangerous. The longing to be ashore is so overwhelming that judgement is no longer reliable. This takes many forms – from holding on to sail too long in order to get ashore quicker, running down to a shallow lee shore when it is wiser to stay in deeper water, even falsely identifying a buoy. There is a desperate longing to identify the next navigation buoy as the one hoped for – sometimes in spite of the lettering painted there!

It is best to delay the onset of seasickness as long as possible. There are some natural remedies which are very effective. It is a motion illness, so the head in the open air (or is it the stability of the horizon?) is very effective, and so is responsibility. A person with little experience and nothing to do succumbs very quickly. There are now many more anti-seasickness drugs available than when we started. The principle of selection is the same as then – the advice of a good pharmacist who has a boat; a selection of pills to try ashore; then reject any that have side effects and hope that one of those remaining actually works at sea. We lacked choice as Dramamine was the only one available.

Sailing along the south coast Margaret protested that she had not been seasick all the way round the south east of England until we came to Portland Bill. We took the narrow passage inshore of the Race, and although conditions were no worse than slight she was seasick. She concluded it was caused by the anxiety of approaching these dangerous overfalls.

Food

Food, its preparation, type and quantity, deserves a great deal of investigation. One needs to double the calories normally needed when working ashore. I find that two hot meals a day are essential, one during the evening and the other after dawn when one is most deeply chilled. Two cold snacks are eaten between the hot ones, usually cheese or hard-boiled eggs, followed by dates and fruit.

Water can be a problem. It should be carried in more than one container – in the event of leakage only part is lost instead of all. We carry our water in four 1-gallon (5-litre) containers, and use 1 pint (0.60 litres) per person per day, but at the same time we also have other liquids in the form of tinned soups and in fruit. Dehydrated meals are very convenient when coastal cruising but at sea use an alarming amount of water and complicate water control.

Hot food, to obtain the maximum benefit from it, should be eaten as hot as possible. We eat all our food from deep insulated mugs – the insulation keeps the food hot down to the last mouthful, and the depth prevents the contents jumping out. These are a tremendous improvement on our previous china and aluminium plates and cups. Glucose and vitamin tablets supplement our mainly tinned diet of soups, thick stews and meat.

Stove

The petrol stove works well. Paraffin (kerosene) is safer but I use the Optimus petrol stove because it is the only stove small enough to fit into the base of the swinging oven and still leave room for two mess tins above. Also petrol can be easily obtained wherever one lands, and only one type of fuel has to be carried. With kerosene stoves a second fuel is necessary for preheating and it is not always possible to change over successfully when judgement is blurred by cold and seasickness. We carry ½ a gallon (2.5 litres) of petrol for a cruise of two weeks, and this gives us ample reserves.

Sails

Our sails are the standard racing ones – mainsail, small jib, and genoa. I can see no reason for using cut-down sails as 70% of any cruise is spent under full sail and it is easier to reef rather than change sail for the remaining 30%. (Occasionally it is very pleasant, too, to be able to outdistance the small racing dinghies that will insist on comparing performance!) We do not use any mechanical form of reefing. The standard square gooseneck is simple, reliable, efficient and resistant to salt water and sand.

We have benefited enormously as time has gone on from hi-tech material as plastic and man-made fibres have since revolutionised sailing. My first two boats (the 'damn tin boat' and the Hornet) had cotton sails which, when new, required careful stretching in light winds, and even when 'run in' the halyards and outhaul had to be slacked each time it rained to prevent them permanently damaging the sails by pulling them out of shape. Windows in sails were unknown and sail fittings such as cleats, pulleys, fairleads were of wood, bronze or gunmetal, and needed frequent varnishing or polishing. Soft and hard plastic had not reached the market, and stainless steel was a rarity and very expensive.

Sail balance

It took me a long time to appreciate the importance of balancing sails. Properly balanced a boat will sail herself on almost any course (except running) with feather light helm. Some of our most exciting sailing has been planing effortlessly for long distances once we had

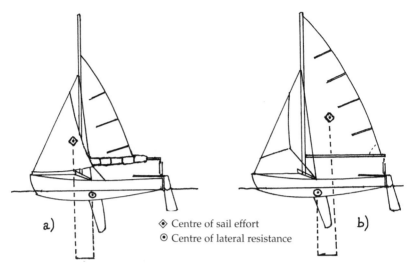

◆ Centre of sail effort
◉ Centre of lateral resistance

a) Turning moment (downwind)

b) Turning moment (into the wind)

Sail balance is important. Properly balanced a boat should gently ease up into the wind with little weight on the tiller.

a) Will fall off the wind whatever the rudder does – but it is useful when broad reaching in rough water as the boat is then well balanced off the wind.

b) The excessive turning moment will cause the boat to pull hard into the wind, making her exhausting to sail, and putting excessive strain on the rudder and its mountings. With a genoa instead of the small jib the boat would be well balanced when close-hauled.

adjusted the foresail, mainsail and centreboard for balance – otherwise we would have been fighting the boat with the rudder every inch of the way.

Furling genoa

Although not essential, this item is an enormous improvement as it takes much of the danger out of working on the foredeck when the wind gets up. It enables the crew to roll up the genoa instantly by pulling on a line, instead of going onto a wet slippery deck when coming into a harbour or up to a mooring. We fitted a reefing/furling gear recently, which enables us to reef to keep the boat balanced (it requires a flat cut sail with a rope luff, but there is another gear that takes the standard genoa). It's wonderful!

Slab reefing

Another innovation on *Wanderer*. After many years using the standard square gooseneck and rolling the sail on the boom, Marg brought back the idea of the 'Jiffy system' from a Canadian Wayfarer rally. It is a development of the North Sea trawler pennant reefing. It is quicker, easier, and there is no risk of damage to the hand if the boom unrolls suddenly.

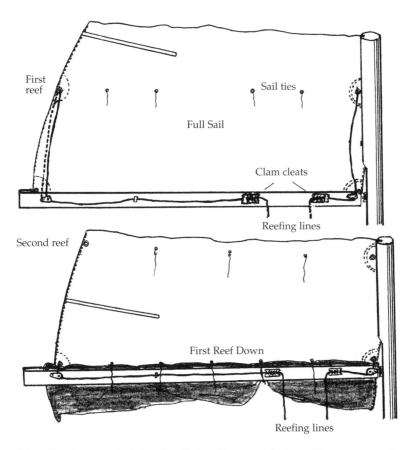

Slab reefing: just ease the halyard, pull the sail down with the reef lines, secure in the clam cleats on the boom, and tighten the halyard. The sail ties are only to keep the sail tidy and do not carry any weight; they can be tied at leisure. It is quick, tidy and there is no twisting strain on the gooseneck.

Running

Running is the only point of sailing where it is possible to push a boat beyond her limit without realising it. It is essential to keep the boat running true with the waves otherwise the result is a spectacular broach to. Marg and I, when crossing the Minch in windy conditions, discovered that it was better to drop the reefed mainsail and sail under twin genoas on the forestay, boomed out. All the sail effort was well forward, there was no tendency to broach, steering was light, and it was possible to run more safely and longer than under normal rig.

Jib and mainsheet jam cleats

Wanderer's original jam cleats were fitted on blocks so that a direct pull secured the sheet. This is standard racing practice for quick tacking; the snag is that an upward pull is needed for release, which is impossible when sitting out a boat heeling in an unexpected squall. On several occasions only the Wayfarer's excellent stability kept us from capsizing and I swore viciously about racing fittings which are so unsafe in a cruising dinghy. Lowering the cleats by removing the blocks cured the problem, as a pull from any direction in an emergency frees the sail.

Lowering the mast

For ease of lowering the mast when shooting bridges, we have fitted a rope tail to the forestay, brought back to a cleat behind the washboard. This obviates the sometimes dangerous practice in bad weather of having to go forward to remove the forestay pin from the stem fitting.

Camera

For many years I used an Ilford Sportsman 35mm camera and found it excellent. It was one of the few cameras that could be used and rewound singlehanded – a necessity when sailing singlehanded with my crew asleep. It was cheap, reliable and definition was good. At that time I was using a separate exposure meter but this was slow and cumbersome, and many good pictures were missed through the time taken to get an exposure reading and transfer it to the camera. When it eventually succumbed to the ravages of salt water I replaced it with an SLR (single lens reflex) camera with inbuilt exposure meter. This was far quicker to use, easier to operate, and still gave me the facility to override the meter to allow for reflection and other distortions one gets when photographing at sea. However, it was bulky and took time to get out from the underdeck stowage bags, and I have now changed to a compact camera with 28–120mm zoom lens. It is light enough to hang round my neck and small enough to lie inside my oilskins where it is immediately available.

A cine (or video) camera is not to be recommended, as the extra work involved is considerable. It is necessary to look at everything with the eyes of a cameraman – do we need a shot of this? Will it film well? Does it fit into the planned outline of the film? Have we got a cutaway shot to lead into it? etc. Consequently, much of the spontaneous enjoyment of the cruise disappears. I was fortunate that Shell required a new film so they loaned me a lighter than usual 16mm camera with electric drive, and I was able to use their editing expertise. Even so I was under no illusion about the work involved and it was only the fact that in many years as a customer I had always found them efficient, helpful and friendly that persuaded me. It was a good film, interesting to make, and I hope Shell got value from it, but I would not do it again.

Navigation

Out at sea, tides can be largely ignored as they tend to cancel out over a period of more than 24 hours. I keep a note of course, speed and wind strength, and note any changes immediately they occur, together with the time, and work out our DR position whenever the weather allows (having these written down enables me to check back if I suspect a mistake in the plotting). Leeway can usually be ignored as I find that everyone unconsciously sails a little higher than the correct course.

A direction-finding radio is very useful and simple to operate; the radio beacons are frequent and they transmit their call-signs slow enough to be understood without mastering the Morse Code. The accuracy is more than adequate for a sailing boat. I carry a Brooks and Gatehouse 'Homer/Heron' RDF set as it is one of the few sets workable in a dinghy, because it is waterproof, shockproof and the compass gives a direct reading. We clip the set beneath the forward decking where the crew can reach it easily from his sleeping quarters to listen in to the shipping forecasts. It has been a most reliable radio and the only trouble I have ever had was when crossing to Iceland and this was eventually traced to faulty batteries and not the set.

Shipping forecasts are useful when cruising to give warning of bad weather, and they are essential when running into the coast for an onshore gale then can lead to real trouble.

Astro navigation is now relatively simple using the Air Navigation Tables. I now carry an ex-naval deck watch for time keeping, and a copy of that excellent little book *Celestial Navigation for Yachtsmen* by Mary Blewitt. I only progressed as far as working out sun sights which seemed adequate for what I needed, but moon and star sights appeared quite straightforward too. Using a sextant in a dinghy is not as difficult as I expected, although in a big sea it may be necessary to sail along the crest to give a longer time for taking a sight.

In the 1960s the improvements to navigation due to come in over the next few years would have been unbelievable. My chronometer deck watch had to be wound every 24 hours at the same time of day irrespective of weather, and now even cheap Quartz wrist watches are more accurate and batteries last over a year. Decca and Loran replaced Consol, RDF was phased out, and the US military provided the worldwide GPS system (global positioning system).

Undoubtedly GPS is the greatest advance in safety at sea since Harrison perfected his chronometer. Now it is possible to establish position within a few yards in every weather condition, and in fog particularly it must be a Godsend. It is a mistake to rely on it solely, however. We have often dinghy sailed the North Norfolk coast and the Wash, navigating the swatchways, using only chart and compass; estimating 'distance run' by eye and wristwatch and sounding with jibstick or more usually with the centreboard. Even in small dinghies a GPS is now considered a piece of essential equipment, and it does make finding the channels between the drying sandbanks much easier. The small handheld battery-operated type is eminently practical in a cruising dinghy, but estimating speed and distance, using transits, working out tides, laying a course to make a landfall upwind on an unknown and featureless shoreline, are essential basic

Crew off watch under the head canvas cover. It's impossible to sleep if you get spray on your face.

navigational skills that must never be forgotten. One day the GPS batteries may go flat and you'll need those skills!

Compass

Our Sestrel Dinghy Compass is mounted in the stern, on top of the rear buoyancy compartment, where it is safely out of the way of trampling feet and below the level of the mainsheet too. In this position it can be read by the helmsman when sitting out on either tack, but as it is mounted behind the helmsman it is fitted with a reciprocal reading card in order to show the boat's heading. We carry a spare compass which is illuminated by a 'Betalight' and which fits into the sidebench just forward of the helmsman – this is easier to use when running and sitting in.

Lights

A boat under 19ft (5.7m) is not required to exhibit navigation lights – only to show a white light in time to prevent collision. Small boats do not show up well on ships' radar; lookouts are not as attentive as they used to be; at night-time a powerful torch lighting the sail is not seen; and even a powerful light at the ship's bridge cannot be relied upon. There is nothing to compare with the hand-held white hand flare – but it must be used in good time as big vessels take time to alter course. We have long carried a torch-battery operated red and green light on *Wanderer*'s bows. It can be seen when the ship's lookout knows where to look but it is not waterproof and battery life is limited. The only safe answer is to keep out of the way. So we prefer to sail north as there is less shipping and longer hours of daylight.

A white riding light is a great comfort even when anchored in shallow water out of the way of others. A paraffin hurricane lantern has been our answer, but it needs attention to keep it burning brightly and not smoking. Lack of battery power rules out a masthead light and we have sometimes used a cyclist's front LED light clipped to the mast spinnaker pole ring. It works well but it is not white – more a yellowish green, but it's better than nothing. There has recently been an advert in the yachting press of a canoeist's LED navigation light that is deck mounted, waterproof, combined red and green with an alternative all-round white, which presumably could be hung on the forestay as a riding light. Battery endurance is said to be 400 hours. I have not seen one but it could be ideal. It is advertised by Adec Marine, Croydon.

Flares

Ten white magnesium hand flares are carried in a box beneath the sidebench where the helmsman can get them out singlehanded. We also carry red flares and a signal pistol with red cartridges but we have never, fortunately, had to use them. These are clipped under the foredeck where they are readily accessible and well separated from the white flares to avoid confusion.

Safety

There is a very real difference in approach to what are branches of the same sport of 'sailing'. The racing man's first requirement is speed, and for this he is prepared to take risks knowing that there is always a rescue launch at hand. The dinghy cruiser is usually on his own and his first considertion must be SAFETY – FIRST, LAST AND ALL THE TIME. There is a saying, 'When racing – reef for the lulls; cruising – reef for the gusts' and the reasoning is the same. The racing boat holds onto full sail so that they are sailing at maximum speed in the lulls and accept the risk of capsizing in the gusts. This is not acceptable to the cruiser who makes a bigger reduction of sail so as not to be overpressed in the gusts, and puts up with being under-canvased in the lulls for the sake of safety.

The log book

Hilaire Belloc, the Victorian writer and yachtsman, was one of my formative influences. He taught me the value of a log book: 'Cruising is not racing; write it down and remember it!'

A log book, even a cheap school exercise book, is a piece of very valuable equipment. I have always made up my log at the end of every watch, not only with course, speed, wind force and changing sea conditions so I can check back on my navigation if I suspect a mistake, but including happenings and thoughts. Doing so, I have to admit my mistakes and misjudgements to myself instead of glossing over and forgetting them. It is an exercise in self discipline to prevent mistakes being repeated.

Tide races

To go through a tidal race is the most frightening experience of all, but there are times when a boat cruising along the coast, no matter how careful, will sail into one. The great pyramids of water rise unpredictably and break heavily in every direction, swamping the boat. I have learned that it is impossible to sail through close-hauled or to tack, as the violence of the water throws all the wind out of the sails. Speed is essential to ensure control – once you lose steerage way the boat wallows, drives astern and then a capsize is probable.

By broad-reaching the best speed is realised, and it may be possible to steer round and avoid the worst patches of broken water and reduce the risks somewhat. In bad conditions a rip like Portland Bill will overwhelm any boat. Forward planning to avoid them is the best answer.

Anchors

We carry two anchors – a Fisherman for rock and weed, and a burying type such as CQR, Danforth or Bruce for mud and sand. Weed is a problem. A CQR tends to drag in eelgrass. Kelp can sometimes give good holding, but the long fronds almost always foul the blades of a Danforth before it hits the bottom and it won't bite when it turns over as the tide turns. My standard practice is to give a sharp tug on the warp to 'set' the anchor, and if conditions are likely to deteriorate and security is vital then I will row in a second anchor. Two anchors in a 'V' is an improvement on lying to a single hook because it prevents the boat ranging round and working her anchor out of the ground and possibly dragging. It also stops her swinging into danger in a restricted anchorage. The angle of the 'V' is important – ideally around 90° (less and the boat will swing on one anchor if the wind changes direction; more and the load on each anchor is greatly increased with the possibility of the anchors dragging together). The Bahamian moor, known in the UK as a 'running moor', restricts the boat from swinging in a narrow channel, but is not practical where the tidal range is great. For years *Wanderer* has carried a 7lb (3.17kg) sliding Grapnel (similar to a Fisherman anchor), and a 5lb (2.27kg) CQR which have served well. It is often recommended to carry as heavy an anchor as possible, but when I

Bruce – a burying type with great holding power, provided it can penetrate the bottom. There are indications that it is less efficient in small sizes.

Fisherman – a very good general purpose anchor, excellent on hard clay and difficult bottoms, and better than others on rock and weed. The exposed fluke can foul the anchor rope as the tide turns and trip the anchor.

Danforth – a burying type with great holding power.

Folding grapnel – a temporary anchor that folds small and meets the regulation that a dinghy must carry an anchor when racing.

CQR (plough-type) – a burying type with great holding power.

Rond – ideal for motoring to the river banks of the Norfolk Broads.

Thames pattern – popular with East coast small boat sailors, excellent on mud and sand.

Mud weight – excellent in the soft mud of the Norfolk Broads.

Sliding grapnel – my favourite anchor, very difficult to find. Similar qualities to the Fisherman and it can also be rigged as a grapnel by securing the sliding flukes to the crown.

replaced a lost anchor with a 13lb (5.8kg) Danforth type I found it was such a pig to handle, especially in a hurry, that I have gone back to my originals.

Boat rollers/fenders

The advantage of cruising in a dinghy is that the boat can be pulled ashore to wait out bad weather or for a comfortable night ashore. Inflatable rollers make it possible for a couple to beach a Wayfarer and pull her above high water for a comfortable night or to wait out bad weather. A tackle (the three part mainsheet made up to four part) can be used to advantage tied to a tree or the boat anchor.

There are two types of roller – the heavy plastic ones which do not puncture but dig in on soft going, and the light rubberised canvas type which will roll easily over quite large stones but puncture if slewed to change direction on concrete. They can be tied low down under the front sidebenchs for additional buoyancy, but remember that in this position in the event of a complete inversion they give additional stability upside down. Pneumatic rollers make excellent fenders too.

Outboards/auxiliary power

We have never used an outboard on *Wanderer*. It is said to be a great boon but I am sure it would slow my learning about boat handling in a seaway as it is too easy in an emergency to 'just switch on the motor'. Without it I have to use my intelligence and experience. A mistake in calculating tide times or tide height means pulling half a mile up a muddy drying creek; a missed tide results in a cold night and returning home next morning; misjudging the weather can lead to hours of rowing in a flat calm or a 'pasting' in bad weather. These have been lessons never forgotten and the mistakes rarely repeated.

Rowing long distances can be exhausting, but watch the professional boatmen – they never pull hard, just lean easily on the oars and they can keep it up all day. Sometimes it is useful to leave sail up to catch any light zephyr but the ear is hit by the swinging boom most painfully. The answer is to raise the boom above head height on the aft reef line.

The length of the oars carried usually depends on the length that can be stowed. *Wanderer*'s oars are the standard 8ft (2.43m). Ideally 8ft 6in (2.59m) is better but this restricts stowage space forward of the mast, and are non-standard and much more expensive.

Fog

Fog is always dangerous but a dinghy with her small draught does have advantages as she can sail in shoal water out of the reach of larger vessels.

Navigation in fog is difficult. There is the choice of sailing further out to clear all dangers such as overfalls, tide rips and rocks – and risk collision, or sailing close in and navigating headland to headland. It is easy to become careless, as fog is disorientating and only the compass can be trusted. If the navigator omits to keep a reckoning of distance run, it only requires a headland not to appear on time and the boat is lost, with no hope of fixing her position until the visibility improves.

Fog is dangerous. In deep water vessels are travelling slowly and cannot manoeuvre; small boats do not show up on their radar; they are unlikely to hear a small fog horn such as carried on a sailing boat; and if there is a collision in fog there is no way that they are able to turn back and rescue the crew of a sunk boat. The safest course in fog is to stay in the relatively shallow water out of the reach of heavy shipping. It is here that the dinghy scores over the deeper draught yacht – she can safely go in and ask where she is without fear of going aground – just pull up the centreboard when it touches bottom. She can pull up the beach and wait for the weather to clear or feel her way along the shore, for under oars she is highly manoeuvrable, and being light the tide will sweep her clear of rocks and headlands. Certain coasts permit fog navigation – deep water close in with sufficient visibility to see the bottom of the cliff, and definite changes in direction that allow the navigator to check position. Everything depends on experience and careful preparation.

Crossing bars

Bernard Farrant, yachting correspondent for the *Eastern Daily Press,* was to crew me racing in the Eastern Area Championships at Brancaster. He commented at the end of one race, 'What good boats these Wayfarers are!' and suggested that he had never been over the bar when there was a big sea running. So we went out to sea via the Channel, worked along the bar, and came in. I had picked our crossing to be impressive, but not dangerous – just about 50yd (45.72m) to westward of the Wreck. Any closer to Scolt Head Island the seas were impossible for a dinghy, and even here the seas were a little risky. The first wave picked the dinghy up and we planed in rapidly. This wave was smaller than most, and it dropped us halfway across the bar. The following one could not have been worse – much larger and beginning to crest 50yd (45.72m) away. As it reached us it was 8ft (2.43m) high and breaking; a capsize was inevitable. *Wanderer* tried to lift to it and was beginning to plane on the front face when the crest fell on her stern. We broached heavily with water pouring over the transom and into the boat, and we capsized quickly and spectacularly. I was close by the stern when I surfaced and was able to grab the dinghy. Diana (to whom we had offered a quick sail after the racing) was floating away so I grabbed her with the other hand. Suddenly a rubber boot broke surface in front of me, so I let Diana go and grabbed the boot and tried to pull Bernard to the surface. By his language, I gathered he was the other side of the dinghy and one foot had floated underneath *Wanderer*; I was attempting to pull him underwater and drown him. I recovered Diana before she drifted out of reach; Bernard hauled down the centreboard and had *Wanderer* upright immediately. We started to bail, and soon had *Wanderer* dry. Back at the club several competitors asked how we had got so wet? Bernard lied that we were coming ashore, and had misjudged the depth – and being the representative of the always truthful *Eastern Daily Press*, to my surprise, they believed him!

Late in October John Buckingham and I sailed *Wanderer* along the North Norfolk coast from Brancaster to Blakeney. The wind was WNW Force 6 and out at sea conditions were even worse than expected, the waves 5–6ft (1.52–1.82m). With the mainsail reefed to the second batten and the small jib set we planed diagonally across the seas in an exhilarating downwind run. Heavy and excessive use of the helm was needed to prevent a broach-to, but apart from this we were enjoying ourselves. Little did we appreciate the strain on the rudder.

Running with a broken rudder: a substitute oar blade has only a small surface and has little effect unless the boat is balanced under sails. The reduced leverage also makes for hard work and intense concentration, but Wanderer *crossed Blakeney bar safely by rigging a second oar. John is wearing an ex-RAF 'Mae West' which was our standard bad weather buoyancy at that time.*

Five miles off Wells bar we came about at the third attempt to bring the wind over the other quarter. On looking over the stern I was startled to see the rudder head splitting, and the blade drop out and disappear astern at something approaching 10 knots. As the boat broached a wave broke over us and we shipped 30 gallons (136.38 litres). John immediately backed the jib and we were hove-to, but surging about dangerously and shipping water.

We rigged a steering oar through the tiller slot in the transom and sailed the dinghy into the lee of Wells bar where we lowered the mainsail. The force required on a steering oar was surprisingly heavy, and at times it was difficult to prevent a broach-to; even under jib alone we were still planing. The sea on Blakeney bar was bad and by lashing a second steering oar to the starboard carrying handle we crossed safely. This trip taught me the truth of the saying 'A boat will stand more than the crew when beating, but not when running' and but for having a tough and experienced crew we might have been in trouble. Writing it up in my log book I realised the seamanlike action in such conditions is to run on jib alone, and that one must always be prepared for an unexpected emergency when sailing at sea.

The truth is that these were two most instructive sails, and I began to revise my ideas about crossing bars in heavy weather. The basic safety rule is never to go near a breaking bar when the tide is ebbing, as a capsize will result in the boat being carried out to sea – a flooding tide will at least bring the boat into sheltered water. I always wish I had experimented with towing a small drogue to prevent broaching, or backing in to a beach with a drogue from the bows (with the crew wearing lifelines). It is unlikely that one will get into a beach with a dry boat if the waves are more than twice the height of the freeboard anyway, and there is the added risk that the boat may be driven atop one of the crew by a rogue wave, with severe bruising or a broken leg.

Undertow is an additional hazard. In onshore surf each breaking wave sucks the sand from under a person's feet, making it impossible to stand.

Over the years my views have changed: I don't attempt to cross a bar if it is marginal, preferring to find a lee around the next headland or even anchor in the lee of a sandbank which may cover at high water but still give some protection.

Bailing

Water weighs approximately 10lbs per gallon and runs to the lowest part of the hull, reducing the stability of the boat dramatically. For speedy removal of large quantities of water there is nothing that even approaches the old fashioned bucket! It is particularly effective when the boat is half full of water, well above the floorboards. It is used to 'woosh' the water overboard rather than bucket it. Once the water is down to the floorboards the law of diminishing returns applies, and *Wanderer* has a permanent piston pump on the side of the centreboard case to remove the rest.

Years later I have fitted a diaphragm hand pump (Whale Gusher type) with suction hose taken down to the lower bilge. It is mounted on the side seats and can be slid along to a comfortable position and operated by the crew while sitting up to windward.

Self-bailers are very effective. They should always be pulled up once the boat is dry, as even with a non-return flap they still tend to feed back when the speed drops. We saw an unusual type of bailing scoop in Shetland on the local four 'erns and six 'erns where a wooden shovel fits exactly between the ribs and is used by the crew to shovel bilgewater overboard.

Mobility and flexibility

A far wider choice of cruising area is available to the dinghy than to the deep draught yacht. With car and trailer, boat and crew can be sailing several hundred miles away within 24 hours, whereas a yacht may take days to flog her way there, arriving in time to return. Sometimes it is possible to choose a sailing area at short notice and have an unexpectedly enjoyable sail.

Many years ago we discovered that two enthusiastic small boat sailors Don Davis and Ken Jensen from abroad were attending a meeting in London with Ian Proctor to discuss giving fleet status to Wayfarers in Denmark and Canada. Margaret thought a trip down the Thames through London by boat in January would add to their memories of the visit, so we met them next morning with loads of warm clothing, Wellington boots and oilskins. We carried the ebb tide downriver through the City and they were greatly impressed by shooting the bridges, dropping the mast and sails all-standing at the last moment with a fierce tide urging us on, past ships unloading into lighters and warehouses (London was still a major port).

The Houses of Parliament, as we had been anticipating, caused great hilarity, with Canadian and Scandinavian witticisms about erratic winds, blowing hot and cold, squalls of hot air, wind eddies, etc.

Lower downriver they demanded a visit to the Tower of London – whereas we had planned to sail down to the estuary and use the flood to return. So we climbed over the railings, were looked at askance by the man in the ticket office, and spent a couple of hours walking round in our oilskins and sailing gear. We climbed back down the railings in the late afternoon and pushed off into the now flooding tide which carried *Wanderer* easily upriver. The City and riverside lights on both banks had come on, and *Wanderer* was sailing quietly in a black chasm invisible to any watcher on the shore, but from the water it was spectacular. Margaret and I had become passengers as our guests had become proficient at mast lowering, although they did underestimate the speed of the flood tide at two bridges. We pulled out with the tide still running strongly, and after a quick meal drove back to Norfolk. It had been a memorable trip, arranged on the spur of the moment.

Snatched passages

These must only be based on experience and sound judgement. Optimism has no place. They are an inevitable part of sailing, taken for many reasons. The first question must be: Does the reason justify the risk? Then comes the planning: Will the weather remain settled for long enough to get in, and is a bolt hole available if it doesn't? Is there a safe entrance to a sheltered haven at the destination or is there a bar which will be breaking? Will we arrive before dark, and if not is it buoyed and lit or is there a prominent landmark to be seen against the night sky so the boat can run in on a safe compass bearing? Is the gear sound? Inevitably the decision will be a balance between speed and sea conditions.

The Wayfarer

When I first saw the lines of the Wayfarer I thought that here was a boat that looked 'right' and had great potential. Apparently others thought so too, for it is now a large class being cruised and raced in many countries worldwide.

Most importantly this is a completely 'predictable' boat – a boat without any vices. In any conditions from light winds up to extreme, and from full sail to deep reefed, you can predict her behaviour. She is very 'forgiving' and she looks after me when I make a mistake until I start thinking again; very few boats will do this. We were very fortunate that Ian Proctor produced such a fine boat when it was needed. Some years later at Margaret's suggestion he designed the 14ft (4.27m) Wanderer because she felt there was a need for a lighter cruising dinghy than the 16ft (4.88m) Wayfarer. Later still he designed the 11ft (3.35m) Gull Spirit which Marg says handles exactly like the Wayfarer, but is light enough for her to launch and recover singlehanded.

Marg and I find that one of our greatest pleasures is to launch on Sunday and to sail whichever way the wind blows us – we rarely beat if we can avoid it – sometimes up to the head of the river, and at other times down into the estuary or along the coast – things that we could not do in a deep-draught yacht. To watch the sun setting over the marshes, or to listen to the river lapping against the hull while the cattle graze the bank above as we drift off to sleep beneath the tent, or to come creeping over the bar in the moonlight – this is what sailing is about!

APPENDIX B

Gear for a Fourteen-Day Cruise

Equipment
spare tiller extension
anchor and warp
2 drogues
2 pneumatic boat rollers (in bilges)
2 oars
2 rowlocks
2 buckets
sponge
cockpit storm cover
dinghy tent
2 oil bags
2 gal (9.09 litres) oil
pouring spout
bowsprit
mast crutch
ensign and staff

Navigational
set of charts
radio beacon chart
consul lattice chart
Admiralty *Pilot*
spare compass
parallel rule
DF Homer-Heron set
2 rubber torches
bow light
batteries
dividers
sextant
deck watch
air almanac
navigational tables
navigation book
log book

Medical and safety
medical kit
seasick pills
splints
2 lifejackets
2 safety lines
20 white hand flares
Very pistol
20 Very cartridges (red)

Cooking
stainless oven
2 mess tins
1 petrol stove
cutlery
saucepan tongs
2 insulated mugs
2 lemonade bottles (for petrol)
spare petrol stove
tin opener and spare
3 boxes lifeboat matches
mop
scourer
spare cutlery
spare mug
4 x 1 gal (4.55 litres) fresh water
9 soups
14 self-heating soups
14 self-heating cocoa drinks
4 spaghetti
7 steak/veg casserole
3 beef slices in gravy
2 Oak ham
2 tuna
2 crab
4 corned beef

3 grapefruit
3 lifeboat biscuits
3 portioned cheese
2 compressed dates
2 raisins/sultanas
3 rum-flavoured fudge
2 large choc bars
14 pkts glucose energy tablets
3 doz fresh eggs
3 large loaves
1 chicken
2lb (9.072gm) butter
3 doz apples
salt
Kendal mint cake
1 bottle whisky

Clothes and personal effects
2 oilskins with hoods (one piece)
2 prs rubber boots
shackle tool
knife
sleeping bags
shaving kit
3 toilet rolls
spare glasses
camera, 35mm
4 cassettes 35mm film
dictionary
2 air beds
wool pyjamas
string vest
long wool pants and vest
padded underclothes
corduroy trousers
canvas smock
2 prs wool socks
towel
wool hat
wool gloves

Spare clothing
2 long wool pants and vests
padded trousers

padded jacket
3 jerseys
2 prs trousers
3 prs socks
12 handkerchiefs
oilskins

Shore dress
1 golf jacket
1 pr trousers
1 pr shoes
1 shirt (white) and collars
1 tie

Fishing
1 trace mackerel hooks
1 mackerel spinner
1 weight
1 fishing line
1 swivel

Miscellaneous
sail-repair box
sailcloth
3 stainless needles
sewing thread
1 bobbin
whipping twine
toggles
copper wire
buoyancy repair
spare shackles
3 bulldog wire grips
screw, clevis pins, split pins
drills
lashing line
plywood for patching
5cwt (294.01kg) terylene line
10cwt (508.02kg) terylene line

APPENDIX C

The Wayfarer Design

by Ian Proctor

At the time of being asked to produce the design that became the Wayfarer Class, I was very much involved in designing (and racing) flat-out high-performance racing dinghies, mostly in the development classes such as International 14, Merlin-Rocket and National 12. I enjoyed these uncompromising racing boats enormously, both the designing and the racing of them, and was one of a happy band of fanatics that competed in three or four different class championships each year.

Our concentration on racing was fairly intense. Launch the boat, sail out to the starting line, race round the course, sail straight back. It really did not matter whether the course had a back-cloth of outstandingly beautiful coast, or if it was on a flooded gravel pit behind the gas works. What you looked for was boat speed, wind shifts, streaks of current, your main rivals, the next buoy, the finishing line. The competition was the thing. The boats were highly efficient racing machines, and of limited use as anything else.

My wife had often told me of her girlhood dinghy cruising exploits in the Solent and I realised we were missing a good deal by being confined to competitive sailing. One evening, as I was tinkering with my boat on the shore at Hamble, a dinghy sailed up the river flowing crimson in the setting sun, picked up a mooring, rigged a tent cover over the boom and before long two figures were silhouetted against the lamplight inside, obviously concocting supper, the savoury sizzling smells of which drifted ashore and made me feel I hadn't eaten for a week. Later they came ashore and told of their cruise. It sounded wonderful.

It was certainly true at that time that though there seemed to be new classes of racing dinghy appearing every month, there were no

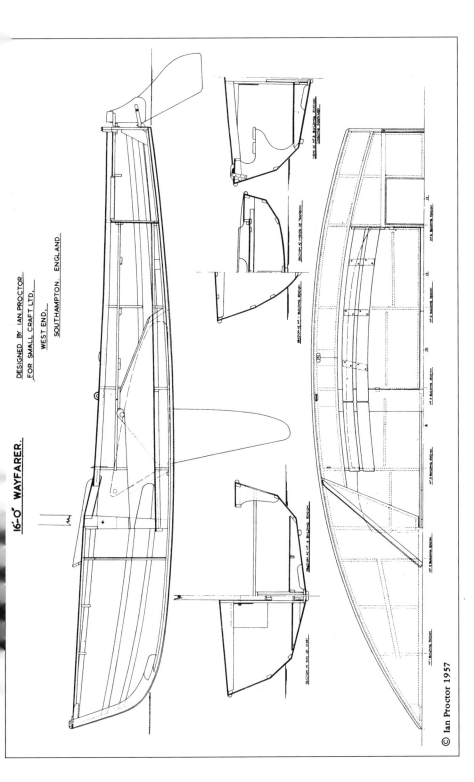

16'-0" WAYFARER.

DESIGNED BY IAN PROCTOR.
FOR SMALL CRAFT LTD,
WEST END,
SOUTHAMPTON. ENGLAND.

new easily built designs to take the place of the many old pre-war local classes of tough, rather heavy dinghies that could lie safely on moorings and take more or less whatever the elements presented to them.

Here then was the opening for the new boat I had been asked to design. A true family dinghy that was robust enough to lie afloat all the time, that would be forgiving and not demanding great physical strength and agility from the crew. Safe, and reassuring for the inexperienced. A boat that could really take all the family in reasonable comfort. A dinghy to go places, that would take your pots and pans, sleeping bags, food and shelter, with a large dry, flat area on which to sleep. A boat that would hide away an outboard engine out of sight and mind when it was not wanted, but which could use it properly when necessary. A mast that could be raised and lowered easily from the cockpit, so that rivers and inland waters could be explored.

This is what the Wayfarer design is all about, with its robust and beamy hull, its fore-and-aft buoyancy tanks that can be used for dry stowage of cruising gear, its flat, raised, draining cockpit floor, its pivoted mast lowering in a tabernacle, its sidebenches that can be removed and swung round athwartships to provide more sleeping space on the floor as well as greater night-time stowage, its sunken self-draining aft deck.

And when we came to think of a name for this boat, I called her the Wayfarer, for that was what she was primarily intended to be. A wanderer, a stroller from place to place.

Of course it was natural that, having designed so many racing boats, I wanted to give this one a reasonable and interesting performance. It seemed to me that, though her weight would be against her, many of the other hull design features that made for speed could also be adapted to produce sea-kindliness, and forgiving handling characteristics. By no stretch of the imagination could the Wayfarer be thought of as a hot-rod – indeed that would be the opposite of my intention – but she is no tortoise either and the performance is certainly good enough to provide interesting and exciting competitive sailing. That being so, it naturally followed that a strong racing contingent formed and the Wayfarer is now raced internationally.

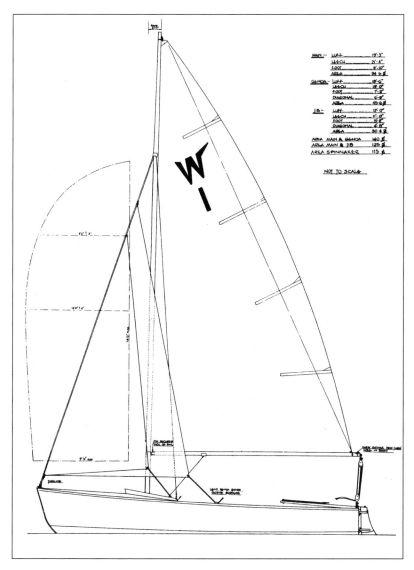

It is inevitable that pressures should be exerted by racing enthusiasts, through the very active Wayfarer Owners Associations, seeking to upgrade the performance of the boat in ways which seem obvious, simple and straightforward to those whose main or only interest in sailing is in racing. But I have throughout been determined

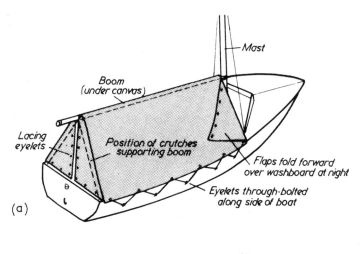

(a)

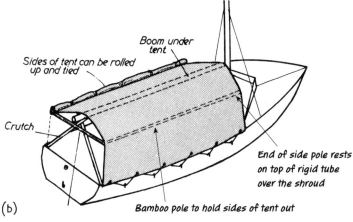

(b)

a) Ridge tent: easy to fit and no extra equipment to be carried.

b) Improved frame tent: increases headroom enormously. Extra side ridge poles and spreaders have to be carried.

The greatest improvement over the years is the use of quick acting Velcro strip when it became available, to replace rope lacing and eyes and hooks: Velcro strips sewed onto the inside of the tent secure to a skirt line fixed permanently under the rubbing strake. Velcro also now secures the front and rear tent flaps, and we have fitted a side door/window for easier access.

Professionally made tents and material advice are now available from a Wayfarer enthusiast – Rob Wagstaffe, Wayfarer Tent Maker, The Canvas Windmill, 38 Castle Road, Wootton, Woodstock, Oxon OX20 1EG. Tel 01993 811027.

that the conception of the Wayfarer shall remain unchanged – and in this the class in general has given its full support. There is a multitude of out-and-out racing classes, but only one class with the special versatile characteristics of the Wayfarer. I want it always to be possible for the owner of a Wayfarer who normally cruises or day-sails to be able to take his boat, unmodified, to a regatta and race more or less on even terms with habitual racers. The class rules have been framed and maintained to preserve this ideal – and so we still have the unique versatility of the Wayfarer, which on the one hand can weather the inhospitably howling North Atlantic, and on the other provides satisfying racing in varied conditions, as well as normal family sailing. Every year, also, thousands of people of all ages are introduced to sailing by Wayfarers which are so widely used by sailing schools.

No one would dare to classify some of Frank Dye's exploits as happy, carefree sailing, but on the whole the Wayfarer is a happy, carefree boat. Long may it remain so for those who sail in it. If this happens, then its design will have achieved its main objective.

APPENDIX D

Reference Diagrams

Bearing of an Object Relative to the Boat   **Boat Heading Relative to the Wind**

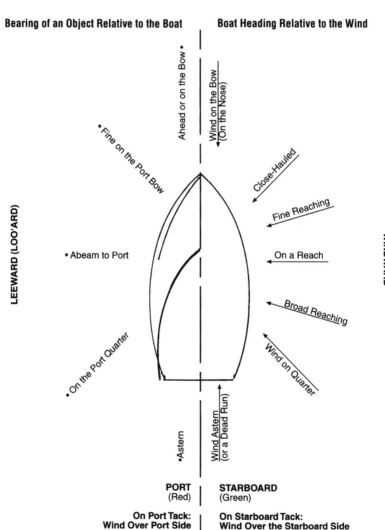

LEEWARD (LOO'ARD)

• Ahead or on the Bow

Fine on the Port Bow

• Abeam to Port

On the Port Quarter •

• Astern

Wind on the Bow (On the Nose)

Close-Hauled

Fine Reaching

On a Reach

Broad Reaching

Wind on Quarter

Wind Astern (or a Dead Run)

WINDWARD

PORT
(Red)

STARBOARD
(Green)

On Port Tack:
Wind Over Port Side

On Starboard Tack:
Wind Over the Starboard Side

Parts of a Wayfarer

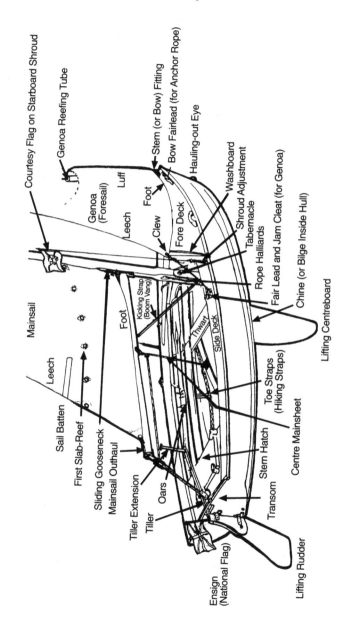

Courtesy Flag on Starboard Shroud
Genoa Reefing Tube
Stem (or Bow) Fitting
Bow Fairlead (for Anchor Rope)
Hauling-out Eye
Washboard
Shroud Adjustment
Tabernacle
Fair Lead and Jam Cleat (for Genoa)
Chine (or Bilge Inside Hull)
Rope Halliards
Fore Deck
Clew
Foot
Luff
Leech
Genoa (Foresail)
Kicking Strap (Boom Vang)
Foot
Mainsail
Thwart
Side Deck
Lifting Centreboard
Leech
Toe Straps (Hiking Straps)
Sail Batten
First Slab-Reef
Sliding Gooseneck
Mainsail Outhaul
Tiller Extension
Tiller
Oars
Stern Hatch
Centre Mainsheet
Transom
Ensign (National Flag)
Lifting Rudder

Index